INCENSE AND CANDLE BURNING

INCENSE AND CANDLE BURNING

The practice and purpose of a simple magical art

by

Michael Howard

Aquarian/Thorsons
An Imprint of HarperCollinsPublishers

The Aquarian Press
An Imprint of HarperCollins*Publishers*
77–85 Fulham Palace Road,
Hammersmith, London W6 8JB
1160 Battery Street,
San Francisco, California 94111–1213

First published as *Candle Burning* 1975
This edition, revised and expanded, 1991
3 5 7 9 10 8 6 4 2

A catalogue record for this book
is available from the British Library

ISBN 1 85538 074 9

Typeset by G&M, Raunds, Northamptonshire
Printed in Great Britain by
HarperCollinsManufacturing Glasgow

CONTENTS

In memory of my occult teacher

MADELINE MONTALBAN

The Light will always shine
in the darkness

CHAPTER ONE

WHAT IS CANDLE MAGIC?

Since ancient times candles have been regarded both as a source of light and a symbol of illumination for humanity. Because of their prime importance in our ancestors' daily life candles became surrounded by myths and legends. Imagine, if you can, the scene in a prehistoric cave: dank, dark and inhospitable. In such conditions early humans had discovered fire but soon realized that its use in a confined space as a source of light was strictly limited. So, in place of fire, they employed animal fat to produce a glimmering light which they used to illuminate the caves and by which they painted the magnificent artworks that were so important to their religious rites. The first candle had been created.

Symbolically, light has always represented the power of good. In the ancient Mysteries practised in classical times it symbolized enlightenment, knowledge and spiritual illuminate. By contrast, darkness became associated in the popular mind with ignorance, evil and the downward descent into materialism. However, the initiates knew that light could not exist without its opposite, darkness; they were two sides of the same coin. It was said that when the initiate into the Egyptian Mysteries reached the inner sanctum a priest whispered into his or her ear the great secret 'Osiris is a black god'. According to the old occult maxim,

'Without Darkness there is no Light and the Light shines through the Darkness'. In the occult doctrine every person is believed to contain within his or her inner self the spark of divine light — the life force — which, by correct moral conduct, can be fanned into the flame of a greater spirituality.

In this way mystics compared the immortal soul to the flame of a candle wavering in the symbolic darkness of material ignorance. A gentle breeze could quench its pathetic light yet, in the stillness and tranquillity produced by spiritual study, the flame rose up defiant and strong. Just as in life, even amid all the troubles and turmoils of daily existence, the spirit defied the onslaught of the forces of evil and inertia. From ancient beliefs such as these arose the practice of candle burning as a magical art, and linked with it was the use of incense as a method of communicating with the unseen powers the ancients believed ruled the universe. The practice of incense magic will be discussed later in this book.

Today people tend to be wary of using the word 'magic', and the practice of magic is seen as a continuation of superstitions left over from the Middle Ages. This suspicion has been created by the centuries of persecution during which the Christian Church suppressed the old pagan religions and condemned belief in psychic or magic powers as evil. There is still a disturbing trend nowadays to equate the practice of the magical arts and the study of the occult sciences with Satanism, devil worship, black magic and all the other nonsense dreamed up by horror writers and the sensational media. With the widespread revival of interest in, and practice of, magic, paganism and the occult during the last 30 years these misconceptions and false images are slowly being corrected but it will be some time before they are completely eradicated.

The word 'magic' comes from the ancient root 'magi'. It originally referred to a caste of priest magicians living in Persia many thousands of years ago. These magi were practitioners of the dualistic religion of Zoroastrianism, which originated in pagan rites of fire worship. In the Bible it is recorded that three wise men or magi brought magical gifts as offerings to the infant Jesus. These offerings included the sacred incenses of frankincense and myrrh used in magical rituals. A magician or magus is therefore merely a wise person who is skilled in the occult (or hidden) arts which are generally unknown to the majority of people.

A famous definition of magic states that it is the science and art of using little-known natural forces to produce changes in consciousness and the physical environment, in accordance with the power of the individual's will. To the magus the universe is inhabited and controlled by forces or energies which have not yet been recognized by science. The practitioner of the magical arts regards the natural world as the visible manifestation of a far greater spiritual reality. He or she is aware of a life force permeating the universe, a force which exists as an energy field both within and outside all living things and even inaminate objects such as trees and stones. Those who follow the path of practical occultism can use this life force or energy to produce what outsiders call 'magical' results.

Candle and incense burning is the most simple of all the magical arts because it uses very little ritual, few ceremonial artifacts or regalia and a form of language which is understandable by everyone. In candle magic the student is not expected to master Hebrew, Latin or Sanscrit or study obscure theosophical and Qabbalistic texts. In fact the ritual tools of candle burning can be purchased in a supermarket and its magical procedures performed in any living-room or bedroom.

Even in olden times, when the practice of magic was often the province of scholars who could read and write, candle magic was a simple and natural occult art practised by ordinary people who had no access to the academic grimoires used by educated magicians. While burning candles for magical ends is not difficult to learn it is just as potent as the words of power and theatrical rites practised by those who follow the path of High Magic. An important lesson which has to be learnt by any magical student is that practical occultism is a simple subject in essence which over the centuries has become complicated by mystery-mongering and ignorance.

Most of us have already performed our first act of candle magic by the time we are two years old. Remember those childhood birthday-parties? Remember blowing out the candles on the cake and making a wish? This delightful custom is in fact an illustration of basic magical principles of concentration, visualization and the use of a focusing symbol. In simple terms if you want something to happen you must first concentrate (blow out the candles) and then associate your desire (the wish) with the actual symbolic art of snuffing out the flames. Your willpower and desire for results make the dream come true. This is a similar psychological technique to the practice of magic, except that the occultist believes that his or her will, combined with the invocation of natural forces and the practice of symbolic acts, creates the conditions on the physical plane for magical results to be achieved.

One does not have to subscribe to a particular religious belief in order to practise candle burning, or indeed any other type of magic. You can be a Christian, Jew, Muslim, Hindu, Buddhist, Taoist, a pagan or none of these. Obviously the established monotheistic religions frown upon magical practices and occult beliefs which they mistakenly condemn as heretical or demonic. It is also very unusual for an agnostic or atheist to practice magic, as a belief in some kind of Supreme Creator is essential. I would presume that everyone reading this book does believe in such a concept. Without this simple faith any approach to psychic or magical matters is rendered extremely difficult.

As we progress into the subject and begin to discuss practical matters such as rituals it could be said that the approach to candle magic becomes a 'religious' one, in the sense that readers will find themselves invoking the assistance of angelic beings. Obviously students are free to interpret these entities in terms of their own personal belief system. They may be regarded as pagan gods, personifications of natural forces, archetypal images, saints, aspects of the human psyche or whatever. If the reader feels so inclined he or she can call directly upon the life force or whatever sacred image of the Godhead they worship or respect.

The concept of the Angelic Hierarchy corresponds with many different cultural images which act as focusing points with which the student can identify and concentrate on during the rite. The religious systems created by humankind are to be used to classify and define Divinity. This has always been the case as far as the initiated were concerned. The pagan gods and goddesses, the angels, saints, etc. are anthropoid personifications of the various attributes of the life force or creative principle which permeates and sustains the Universe. These aspects of Godhead are pictured as archetypal images which have been produced by different cultures during history to represent the Divine.

Underworld of the Unconscious

The three keys to practical candle magic are the occult principles of concentration, visualization, and willpower. It is the mind of the practitioner which carries out the initial work and anyone who burns a candle for magical reasons is seeking to liberate and use the powers of the mind. In ancient religious symbolism this was represented as a winged serpent, and can be seen as the royal cobra on the crown of the Egyptian pharaohs who were occult initiates. One of the foundations of occult belief is that the mind is divided into three distinctive levels of operation: the conscious, the subconscious (or unconscious), and the superconscious. This division can also be found in some enlightened forms of psychology which has translated many of the old occult beliefs into modern forms.

In normal circumstances the conscious mind is active during the waking hours and controls our physical functions and intellectual reactions. During sleep, and during periods of physical and mental stress during the waking hours, the subconscious mind takes over. This period of mental activity is characterized by fantasies, unconscious actions and emotional feelings when the mind is awake, and in the sleep state by dreams, nightmares and sometimes visions. These rise up from the underworld of the unconscious where lurk the atavistic images and desires of our animal nature. In a mentally-stable individual, whether asleep or awake, the superconscious mind is also operational. Its function is to keep both aspects of the mind integrated. A failure in this function can lead to nervous breakdowns or mental illness, especially schizophrenia. Although we are aware of both the subconscious and the conscious aspects of our minds the average person rarely has a close encounter with the superconscious or higher self.

In the practice of any form of magic the principal aim of the magus is to sidetrack the conscious mind, which is often too rational, sceptical and conditioned with preconceived ideas and limiting conventional patterns of behaviour, and contact the unconscious. The latter responds not to the intellect or the use of words but to the secret language of symbols, the employment of visual images and the lure of physical sensations. It is the level on which we experience psychic or intuitive feelings, our strongest emotions and such other worldly experiences as astral travelling and telepathy. Once liberated and controlled by the discipline of the magus the unconscious mind acts as the slave or 'genie in the lamp' which will attract towards its master or mistress the benefits he or she desires.

Some experienced occultists bypass the subconscious mind altogether and seek instead to make direct contact with the superconscious or higher self which in old occult books was called the Holy Guardian Angel. Not everyone sets their sights that high, although this magical operation will be discussed later in this book. Here, however, we are concentrating on contact with the subconscious mind which can be used by the magician to bring into manifestation what he or she desires. In practice, occult candle-burning can help the practitioner to gain the love of others, heal the sick in the service of humanity, improve his or her financial position, gain psychic awareness and progress along the path towards spiritual enlightenment.

At this stage, before we proceed to the practicalities, a word of caution is necessary. In common with all instruments of the occult forces, magic is a double-edged sword. Magical power is in itself neither good nor evil; it is a form of natural energy which is neutral. My occult teacher compared it to electricity, which is useful for boiling a kettle but if misused can cause injury or even death. Similarly magical energy can be used to cure or curse. It is the motives and actions of the practitioner which determine whether the end result of any ritual is either beneficial or destructive.

Obviously it will depend on the degree of spiritual maturity possessed by the student as to how he or she decides to use the energy raised in magical rituals. The practice of magic however does include a fail-safe mechanism. If used for the wrong purpose magical energy can rebound on the user and its effect in reverse is far greater than the original impetus which sent it forth. This fact is recognized in the old saying about the power of curses returning threefold to the sender. Foolish people who play around with occult forces or dabble in magic will eventually burn their fingers before they learn the hard way to take the subject seriously.

This guide to practical candle and incense burning has excluded any rituals or practices which are likely to cause harm to the reader or which could be misused for negative purposes. My confidence in the intelligence and good sense of my readers assures me that they will have no desire to pursue the practice of candle magic for immoral or antisocial ends.

CHAPTER TWO

PREPARING YOUR MAGIC

The preparation carried out before any type of magical working is almost as important as the actual ritual itself. First and foremost the student must cultivate a positive state of mind in which he or she believes that anything is possible. The only limitations on this act of positive thinking and affirmation are the limits of your own imagination. The world is quite literally your oyster — if you believe it is. Often people complain that their magical workings have not been successful, and it is often far too easy to blame the techniques, the tools or even the poor old teacher. Upon examination, however, the cause of the failure is none of these but has to be laid at the feet of the student, who has not been willing to prepare properly for the task in hand. Magic is hard work and you have to work at it to get results. It is not for the lazy or the dilettante who will soon fall by the wayside.

Self-confidence is essential, as well as the ability to ease tensions and approach the practice of the magical arts in a relaxed, yet alert, manner. The would-be magus has to open him or herself up to the natural energies flowing through the universe and avoid any inclination to be tense or 'uptight'. Trying too hard can be just as self-defeating as adopting too careless an approach. The discipline of a system of meditation practised daily for a few minutes is often a useful way to provide a degree of relaxation, although it is not an essential prerequisite for magical practice.

As stated earlier, the magical art of candle burning requires few working tools or theatrical ceremonies although, as with all aspects of practical occultism, some accessories are required. The most important of these is of course the actual candles which are going to be the focus of the rite. What are the best kind of candles for use in magic? Size and shape are not really that important except that it is probably not a good idea to purchase novelty candles with shapes and decorations that might cause distractions. If at all possible, experienced practitioners usually try to keep the candles they use to one standard type and size. This makes life simpler, and after all that is what magic is all about. The candles sold in many different colours for domestic use are recommended.

The old magical treatises laid great stress on newness and one often reads of the medieval magus wearing a robe of *virgin* wool or writing his spells on *virgin* parchment. Similarly in candle magic the candles should be brand new and not used for any other purpose. Never, for instance, use a candle which has been lit as a table decoration or used as a nightlight. There are very good occult reasons for this insistence on the virginity of materials in practical work of a magical nature; it is to prevent the vibrations or influences picked up from other sources by secondhand materials from disturbing the effectiveness of your own reasons for burning the candle.

For the same reason some magicians prefer to make the effort to manufacture their own candles. This can be very useful for not only does it impregnate the candle with the personal vibrations of its maker but in the act of creation the magician ensouls the wax with his or her own thoughts, desires and life force. Candle making is not difficult; it is a popular pastime and there are many art and craft shops nowadays who can supply wax, wicks, perfumes and moulds, often in simple kit forms for the novice.

To make candles the wax needs to be heated until it is in liquid form. It is then poured into a suitable mould, either purchased or home-made, through which a wick has been threaded. The wax is left in the mould to solidify by the natural process of cooling. Then the mould can be removed to reveal the newly-formed candle. Dyes and perfumes can be added to the wax during the heating and cooling process to provide the correct colours and scents for a particular magical ritual. Often craft shops can offer do-it-yourself books providing instructions on how to make candles. Not only is the effort worthwhile from a magical point of view but candle making can also be a profitable hobby.

Having obtained your candles you are ready to perform your first magical ritual. To many people the idea of practising any type of ritual is a daunting prospect for traditionally this is the function of a priest in our society. The established religions, at least until the recent evangelical movement, have not encouraged a high level of personal participation in ritual. In fact the purpose of ritual is quite simply to provide a structure in which the magical principles previously outlined can be practised. Lighting a fire or brewing a cup of tea can become a ritual and the Japanese have exalted the tea ceremony to a religious level.

Before beginning the ritual it is essential to select a place which is suitable for performing your magical working. An elaborately furnished temple is not necessary, unless you are lucky enough to have the space for one in a spare room of your house. An ordinary room will be adequate, providing there is enough space to operate in (space is important because fire can be a dangerous element to work with). Privacy is also essential so make sure you will not be disturbed and take the telephone off the hook before proceeding

Silence is Essential

Wherever you choose to work silence is essential, except where you want to use music of your own choice for mood-enhancement. Candle magic requires a great deal of concentrated effort and this is not possible if there is loud background noise. There is nothing worse than having your concentration shattered by a ringing telephone, a passing bus or a gang of football supporters celebrating outside your window. The presence of small children in the vicinity or untrained animals in the actual room are also obvious distractions which need to be avoided.

It is also a good idea to make sure the room is well ventilated and neither too hot nor too cold. This may seem a rather silly precaution but if you have to spend an hour or so engaged in occult work in a confined space, with candles and incense burning, a certain degree of personal comfort is required for good results.

Personally I have never subscribed to the 'fasting and flogging' school of thought which ordains that to achieve magical results you must subject your body to torture and physical discomfort. However, it is obviously not a good idea to attempt any occult or psychic work immediately after eating a heavy meal or drinking alcohol, both of which make you mentally sluggish and physically tired at a time when you need to be clear-headed and alert.

Many magicians prefer not to eat at all for several hours before a working; others adopt a vegetarian or vegan diet excluding animal products and alcohol. This however is a matter for personal choice rather than an occult doctrine. A ban on sexual activity for 24 hours before a magical ritual is also considered beneficial by experienced occultists. It helps to 'charge up' the psychic batteries which are depleted by lovemaking. Although sexual energy can be used for magical purposes it is not a practice traditionally associated with candle burning. Usually the magus will also take a bath before commencing a ritual. This is a symbolic act which washes away negative thoughts and outside influences as well as cleaning the body. Symbolically it also cleanses the aura, or energy field around the body.

Special clothing is not that important providing that whatever you wear is functional, loose fitting, clean and comfortable. Some occultists prefer to wear specially-made ritual robes which represent a 'cutting off' from the outside world. Robes can be bought from occult suppliers, or you can make your own using a kaftan-type design with an optional hood for meditation purposes. Some practitioners prefer to work skyclad (or naked) believing that the natural life force of the body is weakened by clothes. Artificial fabrics such as nylon certainly can impede the energy force emanating from the body, unlike natural substances such as wool, silk or cotton. However, the thought of hot wax spluttering everywhere may be a powerful argument for keeping your clothes on!

Incense can also be burnt during candle magic rituals to help create a suitable atmosphere and to act as an agent to stimulate the mental, emotional and psychic senses. You can combine incense and candle burning by buying or making wax candles to which perfume or incense grains have been added. We will be examining the various incenses and their corresponding uses in more depth later in the book.

Before beginning the ritual one of the most important stages in candle burning is the 'dressing' or oiling of the candles. This rather peculiar practice has been an essential aspect of candle magic for centuries. The idea behind it is to forge a psychic link between the candle and the magus by using the important sensory experience of touch. By the act of physically oiling the candle you are passing into it, through your hands, your own vibrations and charging it with your life force. In effect the candle is becoming an extension of your own personality and willpower, which is the true function of any magical tool. For the purpose of dressing a candle it is regarded as a psychic magnet having a 'north pole' and a 'south pole'. When anointing the candle, the practitioner rubs the liquid gently into the wax starting at the top, or north end, and working downwards to the halfway point. All the time the oil is brushed in a downward direction. The process is then repeated in reverse, beginning at the bottom, or south end, and working upwards to the middle of the candle.

As the practice of occult candle-burning is a rather neglected art the student will have to rely on natural oils or perfumes to complete the dressing part of the ritual. In recent years occult suppliers have begun to sell candle oils. Many of these are highly priced and the buyer is really only paying for an occult image, expensive packaging and commercial marketing costs. It is better to use your own common sense and inventiveness to find a suitable range of non-inflammable oils for dressing purposes.

While you are oiling the candle concentrate your mind on the purpose of the working. Focus on the reasons for the ritual, visualize its end result, and see your desires accomplished. By doing this you are unconsciously projecting your thoughts into the ether, and thoughts are living forms which have wings. By building up an astral image of what you want to happen a blueprint is created for the reality which will be achieved by your efforts.

Projected Thought-forms

Magical energy is concentrated, focused and channelled by the magus using images which are at first created in the imagination or the astral realm. When the magician directs this energy the image he or she has created takes on a physical reality in the material world.

Every architect's dream house, every author's bestseller, and every painter's Old Master was first conceived in the imagination, the mind of the artist. Thus every completed act and attained result of a magical working must be conceived, practised and finalized in the mind of the magus. The ritual actions he or she employs are specifically designed to act as solidifying agents, making concrete the projected thought forms which are sent forth from the mind of the candle burner. In essence a ritual acts as the turbo-thrust which projects the thought form created by the imagination into physical manifestation on the material plane of existence. However, as we shall see in the next chapter, this process can be aided by outside forces and assisted by a knowledge of the law of magical correspondences.

CHAPTER THREE

ASTRAL COLOURS AND ASTROLOGICAL SIGILS

Having prepared both yourself and the candles, the next step is to decide for exactly what purpose you are going to work magic. It is supposed to be an old rule of occultism that you should never work magic for personal reasons or to help yourself in any way. In my experience this adage is old-fashioned; today the aim of practical occultism is 'to know in order to serve'. But how can you help others in the service of humanity if you are not in a position to offer the necessary assistance?

My occult teacher used to tell me that a beggar is no use to another beggar; both face similar problems and obstacles without possessing the necessary weapons to fight against the overwhelming odds. However, if one beggar can manage to better himself and rise out of the gutter he can return later when he is established and help his former colleague. Not, of course, by giving him a free hand-out, but by encouraging him to follow his example and rise up to overcome his predicament.

This may be a crude example to give as an illustration of how to use magical power, but the object of all forms of practical occultism is to emphasize the individual's responsibility for his or her own destiny. Those occult schools which say that magic should not be used to improve the physical circumstances of the practitioner or better the general lot of humanity are the ones which wish to keep esoteric knowledge confined to an elite so that they can control and rule those less fortunate.

Candle magic can be used for a number of different purposes. These range from overcoming bad habits, attracting love or money, settling disturbed atmospheres, protection against negative forces, regaining health, developing psychic powers, exorcizing the spirits of the departed and so on. You can see from even this short list, that not all the end results can be classified as self-centred. Anything you ask for yourself can be petitioned for another person by inserting his or her name at the appropriate stage of the rite.

Colour Magic

One of the most important and powerful factors in candle burning is the actual colour of the candle. Recent scientific research has indicated that colour plays an essential role in our daily lives even though few people are aware of its subtle influence. We often speak of having 'the blues', being in a 'black mood', or having a row and 'seeing red'. All these common expressions have their roots in the occult significance of colours and their link with human emotions and desires. Colour can be used to isolate and describe specific psychological reactions of happiness, misery, anger and depression.

In fact colours are shades of light vibrating at different frequencies. Red and black may vibrate at a slower rate than, say, white or blue so they register on the human optical scale as 'darker' colours or shades of light. Because of this they will send different signals to the brain of the observer causing different degrees of mental reaction. Some colours obviously have a more soothing effect while others are more stimulating, causing emotional effects ranging from excitement to irritability.

Tests carried out in hospitals have proved that the recovery rate of patients is increased considerably if they are placed in wards painted green or blue. If they are in rooms decorated in dull colours like beige, grey or brown this trend is reversed. We also feel happy on days when the sun is shining and the natural colour scheme is predominantly blue and green while people are more likely to be depressed on dull, cloudy days when shades of grey, brown and black are more in evidence.

Because of the different effects of colour on the human psyche and the surrounding environment different coloured candles are used for different magical end-results. These colours and their vibrations are also closely linked with the cosmic forces which in this book are personified by the Planetary Angels. Each colour in the spectrum is connected with the astrological signs of the Zodiac and their planetary rulers. Below I have listed the main colours used in candle magic together with their magical significances and the influences of each astrological sign.

White   represents purity, spirituality and peace. In some cultures it is the colour of death and mourning.

Red   symbolizes health, energy, strength, sexual virility, courage and the masculine principle in Nature.

Pink   is associated with romantic love, affection and friendship.

Yellow   is the colour of the intellect, the powers of the creative imagination, memory, communication and mental agility.

Green   equals abundance, fertility, good luck and harmony.

Blue   is the colour of healing, truth, inspiration, higher wisdom, occult power and psychic protection, understanding, good health and the feminine principle in Nature.

Purple   symbolizes success in financial affairs, psychic ability of a highly-developed form, idealism and spiritual power.

Gold   attracts positive influences and is connected with justice and career matters.

Silver   represents clairvoyance, astral energies and channelling, also the faculty of far memory and remembering past lives.

Astrologically, the colours and their correspondences are classified and related as follows.

Aries   (March 21–April 20) Ruling planet — Mars. Shades of red, usually the darker shades of scarlet or crimson. Magically the planet Mars is the purifier and destroyer who sweeps aside the stagnant, the unwanted and the redundant so progress can be made. Alternatively, the planet of war also represents the creative principle and the unconscious urge for the human species to reproduce itself, for life and death are two aspects of the same energy.

Taurus   (April 21–May 21) Ruling planet — Venus. Green, ranging from the palest apple green to the dark olive of the earth forces. In magical lore the Venusian energy represents the spiritual desire to unite the opposites and balance the dual forces of male and female. This union was known to the medieval alchemists as 'the sacred marriage' and is symbolized in magic and Wicca by the ritual metaphor of the sword in the chalice.

Gemini   (May 22–June 21) Ruling planet — Mercury. Yellow is the colour of this Zodiac sign representing communication and the power of the mind. In occult tradition Gemini is a symbol of the dualism which manifests from the transcendental Oneness

23

and of the magus who acts as a go-between carrying messages between Middle Earth and the Otherworld.

Cancer   (June 22–July 22) Ruling planet — the moon. Metallic blue and silver are the colours of the lunar sphere. It is the realm of the unconscious, the hidden side of the personality and psychic forces.

Leo   (July 23–August 23) Ruling planet — the sun. Its colours are gold and orange. The sun represents the life force and is the visible symbol of the Cosmic Creator in the solar system.

Virgo   (August 24–September 23) Ruling planet — Mercury. Reddish-yellow is the colour associated with this alternative aspect of Mercurial energy. It represents the analytical abilities of the mind symbolized by the quest for scientific knowledge.

Libra   (September 24–October 23) Ruling planet — Venus. Libra's colours are sky blue and rose pink. It symbolizes the heights attainable by romantic and spiritual love.

Scorpio   (October 24–November 22) Ruling planet — Pluto. Dark red or silvery grey. The energy of the Plutonian sphere is connected with Mars and represents death and regeneration. It has rulership over the underworld, the spirits of the departed and nuclear power.

Sagittarius   (November 23–December 21) Ruling planet — Jupiter. Purple and royal blue are the colours of this Zodiac sign. It is an expansive planetary energy connected with the world of finance and social matters.

24

Capricorn   (December 22–January 20) Ruling planet — Saturn. Black is the primary colour of the Saturnian energy. It rules karma, fate and destiny, the law, old age and property matters.

Aquarius   (January 21–February 19) Ruling planet — Uranus. The colour of this astrological sign combines all the shades of the spectrum in a flashing rainbow pattern. This planetary energy is a higher octave of Saturn and has rulership over magical forces, astrology and modern technology like television, video and computers.

Pisces   (February 20–March 20) Ruling planet — Neptune. Sea-green or indigo are the colours of Pisces, which is connected with the planetary energy of Jupiter. It has rulership over inspiration, matters connected with the sea and entertainment, especially the movie industry.

As described above the use of the correct colour tuned to the purpose of your ritual is important but there are other factors to take into consideration. As we will see in the next chapter, when the subject of the Angelic Hierarchy is discussed, magical rites should be timed to coincide with the particular day and hour sacred to the angel or god ruling the matter in hand.

The phases of the moon are also of some importance in practical occult work. Magicians believe that as the moon's influence increases or decreases with its changing phases it has an effect on magical and psychic energy, just as the moon exerts a tangible influence on the tides, the mating habits of animals, the weather and the female menstrual cycle.

When the moon is in its waxing phase (increasing towards the full moon) then beneficial conditions can be attracted into the surroundings of the magus. When it is waning (decreasing in size towards the dark of the moon) the practitioner can banish negative conditions or influences from his or her environment. The new moon is a time for fresh beginnings or initiating brand new projects while when the moon is full it is regarded as a psychically potent time when astral travel or scrying (clairvoyance) can be practised.

Few occultists will work magic in the period known as the dark of the moon (i.e. three days before new moon). This is a time which is traditionally ruled by the dark goddess Lilith who appears in the shape of an owl. In Biblical lore Lilith was said to be the first partner of Adam before the arrival of Eve and from their union was spawned the elemental realm of elves, goblins and fairies. In reality the mistress of the dark moon has her ancient origins in the bird goddess worshipped by the Neolithic or New Stone Age peoples. Some women find that the dark period of the lunar cycle is when they are at their most aware on a psychic level and can work the best magic.

In addition to the monthly cycles of the moon and the sun through the twelve signs of the Zodiac there are also seasonal changes based on the solar tides which can be used by the aspiring candle burner. These seasonal tides are based upon the natural cycle of growth, decay and regeneration which forms the religious and ritualistic basis of the old pagan faiths. The mark points of the tides are indicated by the spring and autumn equinoxes, when day and night are equal in length, and the summer and winter solstices, which are the longest and shortest day or night. The equinoxes are on March 21 and September 23 while the solstices usually occur on June 21 or 22 and December 21 or 22. The magical significance of these seasonal tides is as follows:

The Time of Sowing: March 21–June 20
The Time of Reaping: June 21–September 22
The Time of Planning: September 23–December 20
The Time of Destruction: December 21–March 20

The titles of these tides are self-explanatory and indicate periods when the magus should be doing workings or arranging his or her life in accordance with the cosmic circumstances. They represent long-term influences and if the magician uses them he or she must expect to wait a while before seeing results. A rite performed at the autumn equinox, for instance, may not come to fruition until the following solstice or even the next equinox, six months later. This is why the use of these seasonal tides is only recommended for long-term magical operations or desires. Those wanting faster results should use the lunar cycle which works on a monthly turn around of energy.

As you begin to work candle magic you will soon find that the equinoxes and solstices operate as changeover points in your life. Important matters will tend to be resolved around these times. Many magicians find the March equinox to be a particularly demanding period. Old friends may suddenly vanish from the social scene to be replaced by new ones or challenging circumstances could arise, leading to a new way of looking at life.

The period from March until the summer solstice is usually a time for new beginnings in general, while from the end of June until the autumn changeover tide the rewards of past efforts can be reaped. From the equinox to midwinter is a planning stage, while from December through to the spring equinox is an outgoing tide for getting rid of unwanted influences, circumstances or social/business contacts.

CHAPTER FOUR

THE ANGELS AND CANDLE MAGIC

Earlier in this book I mentioned the Angelic Hierarchy, or the Planetary Angels, and in this chapter we will examine their function in relation to candle magic. Firstly, it is necessary to place these angelic beings in their religious and historical context before going on to describe their esoteric and magical significance.

We live in a nominally Christian country, even though Christianity in the sense of an organized religion supported by churchgoers is now a minority belief. A large proportion of British people will automatically describe themselves as 'Church of England' even though their contact with the Christian religion is confined to the rituals of christenings, weddings and funerals. In our multi-cultural society traditional religious beliefs have also been challenged by ethnic faiths and the alternative spirituality of the New Age movement and the occult revival.

Because the average person's religious life has been dominated by a Christian upbringing, ideas about the reality of angels are likely to be limited. The Reformation destroyed almost all the occult symbolism and magical imagery which the Catholic Church had adopted from the old pagan religions, so the concept most people have of angels is based on the Sunday-school illustrations of winged creatures in flowing nightgowns as depicted by Victorian artists. In fact the majority of people, whether Christian or agnostic, would be likely to reject the idea of angels out of hand as the product of childhood fairy tales or religious superstition.

This is a great mistake, however, for these great cosmic beings do have a place in reality and can be contacted by those who believe in them. The idea of the Planetary Archangels originated in the belief in archetypal cosmic forces which the ancients in the Middle East associated with the seven classical planets of early astronomy. These planetary energies were personified as gods and goddesses and accepted into the Jewish faith where they were transformed into the archangels.

In the Bible angels are described as messengers between the divine realm and the world of mortals. There are Biblical accounts of the intervention of angels in the affairs of human beings. Several important figures in both the Old and New Testament, including Jesus, have births which are heralded by angelic communications. A less well-known story of angelic contact with the human race is the legend of the Ben Elohim or 'Sons of God' who allegedly came down to Earth and mated with 'the daughters of men'. In the apocryphal *Book of Enoch* the Ben Elohim or Watchers are described as fallen angels who taught their human brides the arts of magic, enchantments, the secret lore of healing plants, astrology, weather prediction, metallurgy, occult wisdom and agriculture.

In Genesis 6:2-7 it relates that the offspring of the illicit mating between the Watchers and mortal women were a race of giants known as the Nephelim who were skilled in the magical arts. Some of these 'great men of renown' turned their occult knowledge to the pursuit of evil and because of their wicked activities they were punished by divine retribution — the Flood, which destroyed all humankind except for Noah, his family and the zoological ark, a legend which can be found in the creation myths of ancient cultures all over the world. It also forms the basis for the esoteric tradition of the lost continent of Atlantis which was drowned beneath the sea because of the evil acts of its occult adepts. The story of the Deluge is also found in Babylonian mythology and it can therefore be assumed that the 'fallen angels' are the old planetary deities.

Occult tradition asserts that among the various gifts passed on to humanity by the so-called fallen angels or Watchers was the knowledge of the use of fire, especially for smithcraft. Candle burning is, of course, the use of the fiery element for magical purposes. In ancient Jewish occult lore the art of candle magic is placed under the rulership of a special angel known as Lumiel. His name when translated from Hebrew means 'Light of God' and he is said to be the first created of the archangels.

Although writers, artists and psychics frequently depict the archangels in humanoid form they are in fact beings composed of pure cosmic energy. The forms in which they appear to humankind are based on archetypal images built up over thousands of years by magical practice and religious belief. The Planetary Angels were responsible for guiding humanity during the earliest period of its existence on this planet and for that reason they are known as the 'teaching angels'. In the practice of candle magic we are primarily concerned with invoking the help of these angelic beings who rule the seven classical planets and correspond to the ancient gods of pre-Christian paganism.

When examining occult traditions and magical lore it will soon become apparent that we are not dealing with many different religious faiths but the symbols and beliefs of one religion which is as ancient as humanity itself and was once universally practised all over the world. According to the oldest and most secret esoteric teachings this wisdom religion was given to the early humans by the 'gods' or 'angels'. It is now known that the stone circles erected by our prehistoric ancestors were astronomically aligned to the sun, moon and stars. It is believed by many that the priest-magicians responsible for their construction had been trained in the old stellar wisdom and that the circles were used for extra-terrestrial contact and as gateways to other dimensions.

The incomplete, corrupted and fragmented natural science which is called occultism — or the study of the hidden — is a surviving remnant of the original wisdom teachings of divine origin. Confused relics of this ancient wisdom can be found concealed in popular folklore, seasonal customs, magical beliefs and rural superstitions. In its own way the natural magic of candle and incense burning is an aspect of the practical side of this ancient spiritual belief system, which is sometimes described as The Old Religion to distinguish it from later faiths which are mere copies of it. In practice every religion invented by humankind is just old wine in new bottles. Today, at the dawning of the Aquarian Aeon, the New Age movement claims to be presenting an alternative spiritual message for the twenty-first century. In fact, in the promotion of crystals, shamanism, earth energy, ley lines, Nature worship, herbalism, and the Goddess, the New Agers are only returning to the ancient beliefs of our pagan ancestors enshrined in occult tradition and magical practice for thousands of years.

The Angelic Hierarchy

The archangelic forces which can be invoked for assistance during the rites of candle magic are listed below, together with their attributes, archetypal images and pagan counterparts.

Michael rules the planetary sphere of the sun. In the old pagan religions he is represented by the solar deities such as Helios, Apollo, Ra and Lugh. In some of the early cultures the solar energy was symbolized by a goddess. As like all the angels, Michael is androgynous in nature, his pagan equivalents can also be solar goddesses such as Brighid or Sekhmet.

The Archangel Michael is a personification of the life force and in all cultural forms, whether depicted as masculine or feminine, the sun represents the creative principle. Michael's archetypal image is a warrior figure clad in a gold cloak and robe. He has amber-coloured hair which flows back from his forehead like the mane of a lion. His hands rest upon the hilt of a broad sword resting point downwards in front of him.

The solar angel can be called upon in all matters associated with career prospects, sport, personal finances, bureaucracy and the health of the physical body. His sacred day of the week is Sol Day or Sunday.

Gabriel is the archangel of the moon. He can be seen in the pagan pantheon as the goddesses Diana, Selene, Hathor and Hecate and by moon gods such as Thoth and Sin, who took over the role of female lunar deities in patriarchal times.

The magical image of Gabriel is a mature man with long white hair wearing a silver crown on which is displayed the curved crescent of the waxing moon. He is wrapped in a silver cloak which reflects the light as if it were made from mother-of-pearl. The lunar angel can be invoked for attaining psychic powers, astral travelling, aiding conception, easing childbirth, healing women's ailments, safe travel by sea and domestic matters. His day is Moon Day or Monday.

Raphael is the planetary ruler of Mercury, the planet which speeds fastest around the sun. In the pagan religions this angel was known as Hermes, or Mercury, the messenger of the gods, Ogma who invented the Celtic writing system Ogham named after him, Odin the shaman god of the Norse people who sacrificed himself to discover the runes, and the Egyptian ibis-headed god Thoth in his aspect as divine scribe.

Archetypally, Raphael is depicted as a young man dressed in the traditional garb of a medieval traveller or pilgrim as shown in the Tarot card known as The Fool. He wears a yellow cloak, a broad-brimmed hat with a feather in it (usually from a magpie as this is his sacred bird), winged sandals and carries a staff. Around this are entwined twin snakes forming the symbol of the physician.

Raphael can be invoked for mental healing, communication, safety on short journeys, anything connected with young people, education, business contracts, commerce, salesmanship or writing. He can also help to find lost property or track down stolen goods. This angel can also act as a spiritual guide on the occult path and as a messenger to the other archangels. His sacred day is Woden's Day or Wednesday.

Anael is the archangel of Venus who is represented by the pagan goddesses of love such as Aphrodite, Astarte, Isis and Freya and by the male deities Eros, Cupid, Dionysius and Frey.

His archetypal image is an androgynous youth with the beauty of both sexes. He wears a green cloak and robe made of leaves and his long black hair is garlanded with a crown of red and white roses. Anael carries a phallic-tipped wand decorated with coloured ribbons.

The Venusian angel can be called upon in all matters pertaining to romantic love, friendship, harmony, the environment, music and the arts. He is the angel of Nature and his sacred day is Freya's Day or Friday.

Samuel is the archangel ruling the red planet, Mars. In pagan times he was personified by the martial gods such as Ares, Mars and Tiw and warrior goddesses such as the Morrigan in Irish myth. He symbolizes the destructive side of the life force and male energy which, when channelled correctly, can be used for positive purposes.

The archetypal image of Samuel is a tall strong man wearing a scarlet cloak and robe. His red hair is tied in a warrior's ponytail and bound by an iron band on which is engraved a pentagram or five-pointed star. He holds a spear and a shield.

This archangel can be called upon for anything to do with physical courage, machinery, craftsmanship or protection from fire and violence. He is the scourge of muggers, rapists and those who beat women. His sacred day is Tiw's Day or Tuesday.

Sachiel is the planetary angel of Jupiter and in ancient mythology he was the sky father god, consort of the Great Mother Goddess. He was known as Jove, Zeus, Dagda, Ptah and Thor and represents the masculine phallic power which brings fertility and material wealth.

Sachiel's magical image is a mature man who is a father figure. He has grey hair and beard and wears a purple cloak and robe decorated with gold coins. In his hand Sachiel holds a royal sceptre or wand as a symbol of his spiritual power. His image can be seen as The Emperor in the Major Arcana cards of the Tarot.

This archangel has rulership over wealth, social status, political power, big business, financial speculation and legal matters. His sacred day is Thor's Day or Thursday.

Cassiel rules Saturn and in the pagan Old Religion he was known as Chronos while his female aspects are represented by Kali, the Fates and the Norns. Cassiel is the Lord of Time and in angelic magic symbolizes the cosmic force of karma or destiny.

His magical image is a stern old man clad in a long black cloak and robe. He carries a staff and an hourglass representing his dominion over the laws of time. Cassiel's archetypal image can also be seen in the Tarot card The Hermit.

This angel can be invoked for anything to do with property, old age, wills, karmic matters, death, land and agriculture and all long-standing health ailments. His sacred day is Saturn's Day or Saturday.

Darker Aspects

Before we discuss the practical side of candle burning we need to look at the darker aspects which cannot be ignored and need to be explained. These darker aspects arose during the Middle Ages when the Church had effectively suppressed the old pagan beliefs and any form of magical practice was falsely regarded as heresy or devil worship. The puritanical clerics condemned the pagan worship of the life force which often used erotic symbols and images, and the heathen temples were destroyed and replaced by churches. In order to dispel the folk myths surrounding these darker aspects of magical practice I will examine some of them in detail and place them in perspective against the background of genuine candle magic.

Occultists are generally of the opinion that the terms 'white magic' and 'black magic' so beloved of the media and sensational novel writers are fairly meaningless in practice. As discussed earlier, magical energy is a neutral force which can be used for good or misused by evil people. The end result depends almost entirely on the motive in the heart of the practitioner and, to some extent, on the methods he or she uses to achieve the aim.

Candles have been employed many times in the past in the rites of what the ignorant call 'black magic'. Perhaps the best-known instance of their misuse is the horrible medieval superstition known as the 'Hand of Glory'. According to folklore, this grisly object was supposed to be the severed hand of a murderer and had to be removed from the corpse at the dark of the moon. It was then dipped in wax and wicks were tied to each of the fingertips. When lit the ignorant believed this gruesome relic had the magical power to render the occupants of a house unconscious and open locked doors. It was allegedly, therefore, much prized by burglars.

Horrific and nonsensical as this now seems, is there in fact any basis to the obscene object? In fact there is, but the Hand of Glory was not the freshly-amputated limb of a felon but an ordinary wax candle in the shape of a hand. Bizarre candles of this shape can be bought today in novelty shops or the amateur can create one worthy of a horror movie by pouring wax into a homemade mould created from an old rubber washing-up glove. Serious occultists today would only want to make a Glory Hand for fun and it is unlikely it would be of any use — even to a cat burglar. There is no evidence that it could render a modern burglar alarm inoperational so its use today among the criminal fraternity would be strictly limited!

Black Candles

Another hoary old occult myth which needs to be debunked concerns the use of black candles in magical rites. No paperback occult thriller about Satanism or voodoo is complete without gory references to Black Masses lit by black candles. In fact Satanism is a Christian heresy which has nothing to do with genuine magic or occultism and Satanists borrowed the concept of a naked woman on the altar at their Black Masses from ancient pagan fertility rites where the priestess was the living personification of the Goddess.

In black-magic stories the candles are often said to be made of pitch and they burn with an unholy blue light. In genuine candle-magic practice the colour black is used quite legitimately in rites invoking the Saturnian or Plutonian energies and in ceremonies for the departed. Blue is regarded by occultists as a very spiritual colour so it seems unlikely any self-respecting Satanist would burn candles of that type in his temple. Anyway candles made from pitch would give off such an unpleasant smell that the practitioners would flee the vicinity coughing and spluttering.

One usually finds that most stories about so-called 'black magic' or Satanic rites are the product of overimaginative newspaper journalists, the religious prejudice of fundamentalists or the fantasies of the ignorant and the credulous who believe everything they read or see on television. Only when the bright light of reason and logic is shone into the dark places of the human imagination are the shadows driven away and the darkness made to surrender its secrets. Nor should we be scared of the dark for, as mentioned earlier, light and dark are twin aspects of the creative principle. Our modern concept of a battle between the forces of light and the powers of darkness, which is a common theme in occult fiction, is a dualist misunderstanding of the old pagan myths based on the death and resurrection motif of the annual cycle of the seasons.

CHAPTER FIVE

RITUALS FOR WEALTH, LOVE AND HAPPINESS

Candle and incense burning is a form of magic which is often called 'elemental'. This means that it is concerned with the control of one of the four elements of fire, earth, air and water. Medieval occultists believed that these elemental forces, impregnated with ether or spirit, formed the foundation of the natural world. As one would expect candle magic and incense burning comes under the rulership of the elemental power of fire and its patron is the Archangel Michael, Lord of the Sun. So before doing any form of practical work with either candles or incense you should petition Michael for his protection and guidance. The following invocation is offered as an example of the wording you could use. As with all the rituals in this book, it is offered as a guide only for often the most powerful magic is spontaneous and comes from the heart. Nothing should be treated as dogma and you should experiment and improvise as much as possible while retaining a recognizable structure to your rituals.

O Great Archangel Michael who is like unto
God, Lord of the Sun and the Angelic Hosts,
protect me in my magical work.

Guide me along the true path of occult wisdom
and knowledge,
lend your power to my efforts as I mould the
flames of your element into creative forms
controlled by my will.

Each of the elements also has a ruler, not an angel but Nature
spirits who control their own elemental force. In the case of fire this
entity is known as Djinn. After petitioning Michael for his
protection and guidance a similar evocation (you invoke
angels/gods and evoke spirits) can be recited to the Lord of Fire
as follows:

O Djinn, Lord of the Ever Burning Flame,
I ask your help and the assistance of your
spirit companions in the magical work to
be completed this day.

Strengthen my will, increase my power and
release the force of the astral light so
that the Great Work can be accomplished
in the name of the Archangel Michael and
his Angelic Host.

While reciting these words imagine Michael towering before you in
the form described earlier in the book. Djinn can be visualized in
the shape of a fire giant as described in the old Norse legends. His
lithe body is composed of twisting, living flame and his slanted eyes
glow with fiery power. He is surrounded by a glowing, incandescent
aura flecked with yellow, red and orange sparks.

A Ritual for Attracting Money

There are two primary desires which play an important part in the
lives of most people; one is love and other is money. Candle magic
offers rituals for gaining both these attributes in workings which

promise the practitioner emotional and financial security.

First, the material angle will be discussed. The love of money may be the root of all evil but many people are willing to risk entanglement by attaining large quantities of this precious commodity. Whether they are actually happier once they possess it is another matter altogether. This usually depends on their character and their general attitude to life. A generous person with only very limited resources who would share a last crust with those less fortunate is less likely to become a miser if given unimaginable wealth and will use the opportunity wisely to help others.

There are few people in our materialistic, consumer society who do not at some time in their lives desire more money then they actually possess, even if it is only to pay the mortgage and the electricity bill without having to skimp and save every penny. Often though the pursuit of wealth can become a curse. Often millionaires with money to burn crave for more and more as if afraid their vast resources will vanish overnight in a puff of devaluation — which, of course, sometimes happens. Although the gaining of financial rewards by the use of magical methods is frowned upon by some occult schools it is generally agreed that the manifestation of modest amounts of money for a specific purpose or in times of dire need is permissible.

The motive, as we have seen, is the key to what is considered 'right' or 'wrong' in practical occultism. Providing your motive is pure, the powers-that-be do not mind your having money or gaining it by the use of occult techniques. However, if the ritual is successful you should return a small percentage (say 10 per cent) to them by furthering some kind of spiritual work with it on the material plane. This could simply mean sending a donation to an appropriate charity, e.g. a hospice, famine relief or animal welfare. The cardinal sin would be to hoard anything you gain rather than put it into free circulation. As my teacher used to say, the occult law is that money was made round to go around!

The acquisition of money is also a karmic process. This is linked with the residues of karma carried forward from past lives and experienced occultists know that money, or the lack of it, is often a tool used by the forces of destiny to teach some of the hardest lessons to the developing soul. If you are not meant to be rich and use large amounts of money in this lifetime then all the magical rituals in the world will not attract it to you. In practice I know of few magicians who are millionaires but most seem to survive and manage to live fairly comfortably.

On the practical side, using candle burning to attract money into your personal environment involves lighting a green or purple candle which represents abundance and material wealth. The working should be done on either the night of the new moon, signifying the beginning of a new cycle, or when the waxing (increasing to full) moon is in the Zodiac sign of Sagittarius, which is ruled by Jupiter, the planet of money luck. Astrological magazines such as *Prediction* provide monthly information on the position of the moon in the Zodiac. If you are more seriously interested in astrological matters you can select a time when Jupiter, or whatever planetary energy you are using, is favourably aspected.

Before actually lighting the candle, sit for a few minutes and clear your mind everyday thoughts and impressions. Breathe slowly and regularly until you feel completely relaxed and your mind is no longer buzzing with everyday thoughts. Let yourself open up and imagine your mind becoming a crystal-like receptacle for the magical energy which will flow through it. To do this initial exercise you do not need sit crosslegged in the lotus position, unless of course you are familiar with this through practising yoga or Eastern meditations. Most occultists following the Western Esoteric Tradition adopt the Egyptian position, sitting upright in a chair with the back well supported, feet flat on the ground, knees together and the hands resting comfortably on the thighs.

Once you feel completely relaxed the ritual can commence. After invoking Michael and Djinn for protection, five candles should be lit in the form of a five-pointed star or pentagram using suitable safe holders. Under each of the candle holders place a small coin such as a 10 pence piece. In front of the lights position five more coins, again in the form of a star. (Those readers who have used the Tarot will recognize this symbol as one of the suits of the Minor Arcana known as Pentacles. In Tarot symbolism Pentacles represent money and wealth.)

40

Having set up this magical pattern with the candles and the coins repeat aloud the following words:

> Money is a necessary evil required
> to make the world go around,
> Too great a desire for its possession
> is an even greater evil that must be
> avoided.

> I ... (*insert your name*) desire
> enough money for my needs in order
> to accomplish the following ...
> (*insert reason*) and to further the
> cause of the Great Work.

After reciting the above words, imagine a pentagram glowing with green and purple light hovering above the candle flames. At each tip of the star a gold coin, like the pieces of eight found in pirate treasure, reflects the candlelight below. As you visualize this astral sigil repeat aloud the words below:

> Archangel Sachiel, Lord of Jupiter,
> I direct my words to you that you
> may grant my wishes and fulfil my
> present need for material sustenance.

> This money that I ask for is needed
> because ... (*insert reason*) and not
> because I am a greedy person wishing
> to live an idle life of luxury.

> Lord Sachiel, angel of good fortune,
> grant me my wishes and send money
> luck to me. So mote it be.

As soon as you have finished saying this petition, visualize money pouring down in the form of gold coins from an upturned cornucopia or horn of plenty. In your mind's eye see the coins cascading through the air and hear them tinkling on to the ground in front of you.

Sit for a few minutes quietly in front of the burning candles. Look at the flickering candle flames and keep imagining the coins spinning down towards you through the astral ether. Allow the candles to burn out. During this period you can add extra power to the ritual by meditating on the Tarot cards known as The Wheel of Fortune, The Ace of Pentacles, The Sun, The World and The Empress, which are all good luck symbols.

When this ritual works the practitioner may find he or she has a small win on the football pools or premium bonds or a salary increase which will provide enough extra cash for his or her immediate needs. Never imagine that magic produces results through any other medium than the physical plane. Although apports are a recognized feature of psychic phenomena the would-be magician who expects five pound notes to drift down from the ceiling after doing a money ritual is living in a world of self-deluded fantasy.

Always remember that a portion of any money received through magic should be returned to the Gods for 'to give is to receive'. Do not worry how you will do this, as they will find a way. However, if you fail to meet your side of the bargain then you may suddenly find yourself faced with totally unexpected expenses which melt away your gains. Like fairy gold it will vanish back into the astral plane and will benefit someone else. This is the lesson behind the distorted medieval tales of the Faustian magician who sells his soul by signing a pact with the Devil for fame and riches.

Great fortunes will never be made through the practice of magical rituals such as the one outlined above, so that the magus can wallow in a despotic life of overindulgence. However, there is no spiritual virtue in poverty and enough money to cater for your immediate requirements is usually forthcoming and is usually the best that can be achieved. Even then part of whatever is obtained must be returned to the sender for the sheer audacity of bothering the Powers with such trivial matters in the first place.

A Ritual for Attracting Love

The practice of any type of magical ritual means that the practitioner is in contact with forces of karma, fate or destiny. It is therefore not something which should be done lightly or without careful thought. In Egyptian mythology it was believed that after death the soul was weighed in the scales of karmic justice against the feather of the goddess of truth, Maat. The soul's good deeds and its misdeeds were then recorded by the ibis headed-god Thoth (pronounced Tehuti) in his role as the scribe of the Gods. The fact that this ordeal faced them after death made the magicians of Ancient Egypt very cautious in their occult work.

Although our incarnatory pattern is mapped out at birth all individuals have a certain amount of free will to make choices and, in some cases, change the circumstances of their life and the direction of their destiny. In this respect one human being has no right to deliberately interfere with the life pattern of another or infringe another's freedom of self-expression.

Often a magician or witch will be asked to do a 'love spell' to bring together two people. Usually this is because one of the pair has rejected the advances of the other and the spurned partner seeks to transform the situation by the use of magic. If the magus interferes in these circumstances he or she is consciously interfering with the other person's free will and this is ethically wrong. However, if the magician works in a neutral way to bring harmony between a quarrelling couple or to mend an existing relationship then this is an acceptable use of magical energy — although often fate will have the final word.

Alternatively, the occultist and the practitioner of candle magic can ask for universal love to be attracted to him or herself or another person. As magical workings are designed only to attract beneficial influences there is no moral reason why a working of this type should not be employed if the end result is the happiness of all concerned.

The following ritual for attracting the power of love should be performed either at new moon or when the moon is waxing in the astrological sign of Libra. A pink candle is lit and before it are placed the Tarot cards known as The Fool and The Lovers.

As the petitioner lights the candle he or she says the following words:

Archangel Anael, Lord of Venus
and Angel of Love,
as I light this flame I invoke
the power of universal and cosmic
love to fill my heart and life.

Happiness and love are the two
hands of the clock of eternal life.
My own life flickering in the emptiness
of the world of phantoms is like the
flame of this candle burning in the
darkness.

Now look at the card known as The Fool and say the following:

As I gaze upon the face of the divine fool,
the adept who stands before the abyss of
immortality, the baby newly born from the
cosmic egg, I find new meaning in my life, new beginnings
and new adventures, happiness flows towards me.

Meditate upon The Lovers and say as follows:

As I look upon the cosmic lovers,
united in the dance of life,
the divine twins whose love
joins heaven with earth,
I am surrounded with love
and attract to myself
the love of others.

Allow the candle to burn out while meditating on the two cards and imagining waves of love and happiness flowing towards you from all directions. Visualize a warm, glowing feeling all over your body. Feel as if you are wrapped in a snug cocoon of loving vibrations.

This little working, simple and direct as it is, will bring new hope into your life, restore your confidence in the mighty power of love to overcome all obstacles and will heal broken dreams.

CHAPTER SIX

CANDLE MAGIC FOR HEALING

Unfortunately we live in an imperfect world and although tremendous advances have been made in medical science, and more recently in the use of alternative medicine, there are still people all around us who are suffering the adverse effects of illness and disease. Modern stress-related ailments and new diseases such as AIDS are but the latest challenge to those engaged in the healing arts.

A considerable amount of time is spent by many practising occultists, magicians and witches healing the sick. As we have seen earlier, it is an unwritten law that those who study esoteric knowledge should use it to help others in the service of humanity as a whole. Candle magic can play an important role in this essential work because it features healing rituals which can restore health and vitality to those sick in mind and body. These rituals can either be used by the practitioner to bring comfort to others or to restore his or her own well-being in times of ill health. As with the money spell in the last chapter, there is no prohibition on using candle burning to heal yourself.

Health matters are generally ruled by the Archangel Raphael, the messenger of the Gods who was known in pagan times as Hermes, Mercury, Ogma and Odin. He has been popularly credited with the invention of writing, astronomy and the Tarot. Raphael/Hermes' symbol is the winged staff entwined with two snakes, which was the ancient sign of a physician.

Healing work should be performed when the moon is in one of the Zodiac signs ruled by Mercury — Gemini or Virgo — or when it is in one of the fire signs — Aries, Leo or Sagittarius. Pisces is also another sign which can be recommended because of its connection with medicine. The waning tide of the moon can be utilized in healing to banish ailments such as gallstones or cancer while Sundays and Wednesdays are good working days. They are ruled by the sun/Michael and Mercury/Raphael and both these angels can be invoked during healing rituals for afflictions of the physical body and the mind respectively.

As we have seen in the original list of colours used in conjunction with candle burning, red is the one usually associated with good health. It is the colour representing the element of fire and symbolizes sexual energy and the life force. When people are healthy we refer to their 'ruddy complexion' or 'rosy cheeks' which are considered a sign of vigour. Red candles can therefore be burnt to evoke the healing power but as healing also comes under the rulership of the Lord Raphael these can be combined with yellow ones.

Healing with Colours

Today the use of colour for healing purposes has been accepted as a scientific fact although it has been used by the priests of the old religions and occultists for thousands of years. The seven colour rays which can be used in combination with candle magic are given below.

Red cures physical tiredness and loss of vitality, bronchitis, blood and heart diseases, hardening of the arteries, colds, sinus infections and sexual impotency.

Orange heals inflammation of the kidneys, prevents asthma attacks, disposes of gallstones, relieves menstrual problems, controls epilepsy and helps overcome mental fatigue and stress-related illnesses. This colour also assists in overcoming sexual hang-ups, emotional inhibition, frigidity, shyness and lack of confidence.

Yellow heals stomach complaints, liver disorders, diabetes, skin diseases and nervous exhaustion. This colour ray purifies the digestive tract and the body's waste disposal system, stimulates the nerves and cleanses pores.

Green can help ulcers, high blood pressure, hypertension, cancer, migraine, venereal disease and influenza. This colour has a general calming effect on the mind and body which is useful in cases involving stress or hyperactive behaviour.

Blue heals sore throats, toothache, dysentery, gastro-enteric disorders, inflamed or tired eyes, insomnia, shock and palpitations. It acts as an effective psychic antiseptic.

Indigo treats all ear, eye and nose problems, lung diseases, pneumonia, infantile complaints, alcoholism, drug addiction and mental illness. This colour rays operates as a psychic anaesthetic.

Violet can be used for neurosis, sciatica, cramp, cancerous growths, bladder weaknesses (including bed wetting), urinary infections and serious malfunctions of the central nervous system.

These rays can either be used in the actual colours of the candles employed in the healing ritual to banish a specific illness or the actual ray can be projected by the magus towards the patient, who may be either present in the room or at another location some distance away.

A General Ritual for Expurgating Disease

This healing ritual can be practised during the lunar cycle when the moon is waning. In this way the health conditions surrounding patients are banished from their aura and astral body as well as from the physical form.

Select the correct colour for your candles, which can either be red and/or yellow and/or a specific colour relating to the complaint under treatment as described above. When the candles have been prepared and oiled they should be lit and the following words recited aloud:

> By the power of this burning flame I draw towards ...
> (*insert name*) the healing rays of the Lord Raphael, Angel
> of Mercury, and I invoke him to banish all negative health
> conditions from the body of ... (*insert name*).

> May the blessings of the great Healing Angels, Raphael
> and Michael restore ... (*insert name*) to full health
> and vigour. So mote it be.

On a plain piece of paper draw in yellow ink, felt pen or crayon the planetary sigil for Mercury. This is an equal-armed cross, surmounted by a circle upon which rests an upturned crescent moon with its horns pointing upwards.

After you have completed the diagram say the following words:

> By this magical sign I place ... (*insert name*) under
> the protection of the Archangel Raphael, Lord of Healing.
> May no further illness or disease trouble him/her and
> his/her full recovery to good health be sure and fast.

The paper is then burnt to ashes in the candle flame and as it burns the practitioner imagines the serpent wand of Hermes surmounted by wings hovering above the flames. The following words are recited:

> This is the healing staff of the Archangel Raphael,
> known among the ancients as Hermes the Thrice Greatest,
> I send this staff to ... (*insert name*) to restore him/her
> to complete health in mind and body.

> May its power support and comfort him/her in this time
> of need and fill him/her with vitality, energy and the
> blessings of life.

Imagine the healing wand travelling through the ether towards the patient as you say these words. The candle or candles should then be allowed to burn down while the practitioner meditates on the patient and, if desired, also mentally projects the appropriate colour healing ray in his or her direction.

Administering to the Departed

It may seem strange to follow a healing ritual for the sick with a description of the way candle magic can be used to aid the departed. However, one of the traditional roles of Hermes, the pagan equivalent of Raphael, was as a psychopomp or guide to the dead, and it is a fact of life that despite the best efforts of doctors and healers sometimes an illness will not respond to treatment and the unfortunate sufferer dies. Some illnesses are of a karmic nature and cannot be cured by healing. In such cases, however, the healer can assist the soul to pass over to the Other Side peacefully and without pain while providing spiritual comfort for those remaining behind.

Death is the final taboo of the permissive society but the practising occultist must learn to deal with it in all its forms. To help the spirit of the deceased make the crossing to the Summerland the magus can perform a simple ritual which eases the transition from the physical plane. This ritual has obvious affinities with the Requiem Mass practised by the Catholic Church, which it adopted from the funeral rites practised by pagans.

White or silver candles should be burnt for the death ritual. Church suppliers can offer fine quality altar candles made from pure beeswax which are ideal for this purpose at a reasonable cost.

Before lighting the candles imagine the departed as you last saw him or her in full health, laughing and happy (if you did not know the person a photograph can be used for this purpose). Then light the candles and repeat the following words aloud:

I light this candle in memory of ... (*insert name*)
who has passed over from the Earth plane to the
Other Side. I/we remember him/her as he/she was in
life happy and joyful among his/her family and friends.

Pause for a few minutes so that all present can recollect the deceased's life before death. Then say the following:

I light this candle for ... (*insert name*)
that he/she may be gathered up by the dark
wings of Azrael, the Angel of Death.

May ... (*insert name*) be carried across the river to be
in peace in the shining place beyond.

Let his/her spirit pass through the gate
between this world and the next and find
true love and serenity with those who have
gone before.

May ...'s time in the Summerland be profitable
that he/she may return to Earth and be united
with his/her loved ones and continue the great
journey to union with God.

Pause to visualize the departed once more and say as follows:

I/we ask that ... be at peace in the knowledge
his/her family and friends here on the Earth
plane are thinking of him/her with love. Go in
peace and may the peace be with you.

The candles are then allowed to burn down in the usual way while those who are present think of the departed person being carried to the Summerland and dwelling there in its beautiful gardens and woods.

Earthbound Spirits

Because of the inadequate knowledge that is available relating to death, and the fear of dying which has surrounded the subject with taboos and superstitions, some souls resist the process of departure from the Earth plane. These souls become what are called 'earthbound spirits' hovering in limbo between this world and the next. Often if the death has been a sudden or violent one the spirit may not even be fully aware that it has left the physical body and may be in a state of extreme confusion as to what has really happened. Such souls will often try to make contact with their loved ones and, if they stay within the surroundings of their earthly environment, can become classified as one of the category of psychic phenomena known as 'ghosts' who are responsible for hauntings.

In a case like this it may become necessary for the practising occultist to carry out what is called in Spiritualist circles 'rescue work' or, in occult terminology, a ritual of exorcism. Unfortunately sensational media reports conjure up an image of the exorcist, who is usually a Christian cleric, wrestling with demons and driving out the mythical Devil from those who are allegedly possessed. As with so many misconceived popular images of the occultist's work this picture of the exorcist is very far from the truth.

For an exorcism white candles are burnt, and if the magus knows, from psychic observation, that an earthbound spirit is responsible for the haunting, he or she will petition the Archangel Azrael, planetary ruler of Pluto and known as the Angel of Death, to collect the wandering soul and guide it to the Other Side. This is one of the tasks of the Angel of Death who in Ancient Egyptian mythology was known as the jackal god Anubis, the Opener of the Way, and in the old Celtic myths as Gwynn ap Nudd, Lord of the Wild Hunt.

Rituals of exorcism can have their difficulties and for this reason they are best left to the experienced occultist, magician or witch who has had training in dealing with the psychic fallout from hauntings and the activities of earthbound spirits.

CHAPTER SEVEN

CANDLES FOR PROTECTION

A popular subject for those interested in the occult is psychic attack and, its reaction, psychic self-defence. The latter term was also the title of a classic book written by Dion Fortune (published by Aquarian Press) which has become a bible for practising occultists dealing with the subject in their magical work. Although written in 1935, Fortune, who was a member of the Hermetic Order of the Golden Dawn and founder of the Fraternity of the Inner Light, provides a great deal of information relating to the harm that can be caused by the misuse of magical energy and psychic power and how to defend oneself from its adverse effects. It should be essential reading for anyone interested in practical occultism or magic.

Genuine psychic attack however is a very rare occurrence although the newcomer to the occult scene will meet lots of people who are being attacked on the astral, suffer from malefic curses or the death rays of an adept of the 'Left Hand Path'. All this sounds very exciting and dangerous to the beginner who is inexperienced in these matters and may be taken in by the wild stories of these occult swashbucklers. However, in the majority of these cases the people involved are in fact suffering from delusions or persecution complexes and could be more easily cured by psychiatric treatment then any magical rites!

Despite this, when a real psychic attack is encountered which has been launched by someone with occult knowledge it can be very nasty indeed. Therefore, as the old but wise saying goes, to be forewarned is to be forearmed. To justify repeating this hoary old adage it might be prudent to share with the reader some of the magical ammunition which can be used to combat 'things that go bump on the astral'.

Candles are a symbol of light and, as we know from dualistic belief, light overcomes darkness. This is of course a rather simplistic way of looking at how the universe operates. It is derived from Christian conditioning and does not allow for the fact that light and darkness are two aspects of the same creative principle. Despite this it does provide the magus with a suitable symbolic model for combating negative forces even though everything is not as it seems. In the Ancient Mysteries, from which modern occultism derives, the candidate's request from the initiator was 'From darkness lead me into the light, from the unreal lead me to the real'. Those who walk the occult path should strive to realize the inner meanings of these words in their quest for the truth.

As light seems to be the most successful and effective antidote to psychic 'nasties' so the best protection against magical attack is to surround yourself with a symbolic circle of light. This can either be a physical circle of lit candles or, if this is not convenient, a circle of blue light can be visualized in the imagination surrounding either yourself or your home. This will provide a suitable ring of protection on an astral level which will prevent negative thoughts and psychic energy from penetrating.

It will soon be realized that psychic attacks are not constant but come in waves over a period of time. This is because the attacker will not possess the required time and energy to sustain a prolonged onslaught. It is a very exhausting exercise to project the thought forms used to sustain a psychic attack on another person. This is probably why genuine magical attacks are relatively rare. Using a mixture of occult knowledge, observations and common sense you will soon be able to deduce the pattern of the attacks. These may follow the phases of the moon or, on a mundane level, even the business or social activities of your psychic enemy.

The circle of protection described above is a very powerful device. In esoteric and ancient religious symbolism the circle represents eternity, which has no beginning and no end and cannot be destroyed. It is also symbolic of the stellar womb of the Great Mother from which the universe was born. You are therefore surrounding yourself with the most powerful symbol known to humanity made from the most powerful force — fire — thereby giving double protection from anything sent against you by those who would do you harm.

The Protecting Angels

Whether you decide to use an actual physical ring of fire or a visualized circle of light you should imagine that at each of its four quarters, or compass points, stand angelic beings. These are the protecting Archangels Michael, Raphael, Gabriel and Uriel (the angel who rules Uranus). They should be imagined in traditional form with huge wings folded back with their tips touching. Each of the angels faces outwards and their hands rest on the hilts of broadswords. Visualize these great angelic figures wreathed with flowing waves of pure gold light and vibrating with inner power.

Traditionally, Michael was the angel who guarded the gates of the Underworld and in Esoteric Christianity he was regarded as the archangel who could defeat negative forces. It is therefore to him that petitions for help and protection are addressed. Michael can be invoked by lighting a gold or orange candle and reciting the following words:

Archangel Michael, Lord of Light
protect ... (*insert name*) from
negative forces.

May your blazing sword sweep aside the
enemies of truth and your golden light
illuminate the dark shadows.

This candle is a small symbol of your
light and the shining presence of your
angelic brethren.

By the token of this sign we shall not
fear the evil sent against us and it
will be returned threefold to the sender.

A second and third candle should be lit and offered as a symbolic act to double and triple the protection surrounding either yourself or any other person you may be working on behalf of by this ritual of self-defence.

When you have completed the petition make the sign of the equal-armed cross on yourself or the other person. This is performed by touching your forehead, middle of the chest, left shoulder and right shoulder with the fingers of one hand. As you draw this cross imagine you are tracing it on your body in golden light. This is not the Catholic gesture but the cross of the elements used since ancient times by magicians and witches to seal the aura and prevent invasion from negative forces.

There are times when unwanted influences and negative forces are attracted to people and these elementals attach themselves to the aura causing psychic damage. The evil that has been perpetrated by humankind over countless centuries has built up into a reservoir of negative energy which unfortunately sometimes spills over into the physical plane. The damage it causes can manifest as dizzy spells, severe headaches, loss of energy and tiredness. Obviously it should not always be thought that this type of symptom signals a psychic attack. Sometimes such symptoms have a physical cause and a doctor or alternative medical practitioner may be of more use than an exorcist or occult healer.

Similar effects may be recorded if the person involved is in the vicinity of a 'psychic vampire' who may be draining his or her energy reserves. Poltergeist activity may be also reported and even the manifesting of entities corresponding to the traditional demons of medieval magic. In such cases it may become necessary to 'clear' the victim's aura and candle magic can be used to achieve this psychic cleansing. The following ritual can be performed, either with the person *in situ* or in another location.

Blue, silver or gold candles can be used separately or in combination. These are burnt to attract beneficial influences and ward off negative forces. Again, the Archangel Michael is called upon as the present leader of the Angelic Host and the magus makes contact with the cosmic force personified by this archetypal image by reciting the following words:

> Archangel Michael, here before you stands
> ... (*insert name*) who is under attack by
> negative forces.

> It is asked that he/she should be cleared
> of this condition, his/her aura cleansed
> and the negative energies dispersed into
> the light.

> I ask that ... be cleansed of all astral
> impurities and attain the purity bestowed
> by the angels on the children of Mother
> Earth.

As you say these words visualize rays of gold and blue light entering the aura of the afflicted person. These rays can be imagined attacking the evil forces in the aura, seen as dark blobs of matter in the auric field, breaking them into pieces and absorbing them. Imagine the person bathed in brilliant blue light from head to toe and looking radiant and happy.

Rite Actions

Do not make the mistake of thinking that the preparation, dressing and lighting of the candles during rituals such as the one described above are incidental to the actual words spoken or the symbols which are visualized by the magus. These simple acts are just as important, for the symbolic mime enacted on the physical plane is in fact linking the practitioner with the astral level, where true magic has its maximum power. Magic and its effects may be realized through physical existence but the real work goes on 'behind the scenes' on the inner planes.

It cannot be emphasized too often that the role the candles play is as focusing agents for the mind, aids to concentration and as symbols of the planetary energies the magician is contacting. To disregard the important position candles have in magical workings is to deprive them of their significance and power to change the circumstances of our lives, on both the outer and inner levels.

Incense and candle burning are ancient magical arts which have endured over the centuries because they work and produce results. If any type of magical practice does not work it will be discarded and will disappear from sight for it is of no practical use to the occultist or magician. Candle magic has never suffered this ignoble fate, although for many years it has been a neglected art. Today, the revival of interest in the occult sciences and the practice of magic has once again brought both incense and candle burning back into the prominence it so justly deserves.

CHAPTER EIGHT

OPENING THE PSYCHE

In this chapter the use of candle burning in the attainment and practice of psychic perception will be examined. It has often been taught that it is only the chosen few who have psychic abilities and that the power is granted to this select elite by courtesy of a divine gift or through the secret teachings passed down by initiates since ancient times. Like so many popular beliefs about the occult this idea is a complete fallacy. In fact we all contain within ourselves the hidden potential of psychic gifts which can be unlocked by a few simple practices.

Psychic powers are our common heritage as human beings dating back to our earliest ancestors who lived in caves. Psychologists are slowly beginning to realize that the average person only uses a third of the actual capacity of his or her mind. It is the exploration and utilization of the hidden two-thirds of the mind which occultists and psychics seek in their quest for new knowledge and experiences beyond the normal range of the senses.

It is believed that in the early stages of human evolution the psi or psychic senses were fully operational in all of us. In prehistoric times for instance the early humans used their natural psi powers in hunting and, before the development of language, for communication. Gradually, as civilization began to develop and humans began to congregate into larger groups the special attributes they used normally in primeval times gradually atrophied. This came about largely because of the rejection of the natural world, and humankind's role in it, in the post-Christian period and has accelerated considerably in modern times. What was once natural has become the artificial province of the few.

In some cases people are born with their psi senses fully activated. These comparatively rare souls are known as 'natural psychics' or 'sensitives' and while some lose their gifts with the onset of maturity, in others it survives into adulthood and remains with them all their life. In other people the psychic potential is very close to the surface and can be developed with very little training. Children will often exhibit a certain amount of psychic awareness but cultural conditioning and education usually leads to its suppression before puberty.

The majority of ordinary people experience flashes of psi awareness at some time in their lives usually during periods of stress, danger or severe illness. There are few of your friends, relatives or workmates who do not have some 'strange story' to tell along these lines. However, as these powers are undeveloped and untrained, the average person has no control over their appearance or use. The proper occult training can help those interested to realize the hidden potential of their psi potential and can also equip the user with an ethical background which can be used as a measuring stick when the powers are used for the benefit of others.

With the magical art of candle burning for occult purposes the main use of the candle in the initial stages of development psychic ability is for meditation. This simply means the practice of 'mental planning', 'creative thinking' or 'contemplation' and it consists of the careful selection of a specific theme, idea or symbol which can be employed as a focusing point to release the hidden knowledge in the mind. This focal point is analysed and examined from every mental viewpoint and angle in order to reveal its innermost meaning.

Some books written on the subject by experts will inform you that meditation consists of sitting still, making your mind blank and thinking of nothing, plus the chanting of special mantras to facilitate this process. Meditation techniques have always been an important aspect of the Eastern religions. However, it is less known that it also plays an essential role in the Western Esoteric Tradition and practical magic.

Meditation can also be the path of mental action for it does not have to be a totally passive activity. To illustrate this point, I sometimes meditate by pacing up and down a room. Perhaps this is because I think better on my feet but the fact is that ideas and inspiration seem to come to me easier when I am actually physically active. This is true 'active meditation' which is an important aspect of the magical path in the West and in some traditional forms of witchcraft.

Clairvoyance and Candle Magic

Through the use of meditation, candle burning can be used to train the mind in clairvoyance (a word derived from the French meaning 'clear seeing') which is one aspect of psychicism. First place a candle on a table in front of you. Concentrate on the flame, but do not stare at it without blinking as this can make your eyes ache and will hinder results. The best method is to gaze at the candle flame for a few minutes and then look away. When looking at the candle you can use the Eastern technique of clearing the mind of unwanted thoughts.

This form of meditation is more difficult then it seems, for the human mind is incapable of remaining in this state for long periods of time without alien thoughts intruding. Therefore use this method slowly in short bursts of concentrated effort and rest. When you begin to feel tired, break off and try again later. Eventually, when you have trained your mind to clear at will, you are in a state to become receptive to any images and symbols it may receive which can be interpreted for their psychic or occult (hidden) meanings.

An alternative method for gaining clairvoyant powers, which is often used in natural magic, is to reflect the light of the candle flame in a mirror, crystal or bowl of water. As those of a romantic inclination will know, candlelight has its own special magic to enchant and transform the mundane into something really special. When reflected on to a polished or mirrored surface the light from a candle can produce some very interesting results. In fact the flame reflected in this way can produce the subtle form of psychic energy which is described in old occult treatises as the Astral Light. In this forcefield images and visions from the Otherworld can manifest and it can also act as a materializing medium for spirits.

Clairvoyance using a mirror or crystal is known as scrying and one often hears occultists talking about 'scrying in the astral'. This term refers specifically to visions received through the agency of a crystal by a seer direct from the astral plane or spirit world. It is interesting to note that in recent years crystals have become popular New Age toys and are widely sold by occult suppliers for their energizing properties. However, crystals were widely used by the ancients for magical and psychic purposes and were also known to the oldtime witches, wizards and magicians who used them for seership and contacting the spirits.

The acquisition of psychic powers in candle magic comes under the rulership of the Archangel Asariel, who is the planetary governor of Neptune. In astrology and mythology this planet is associated with the secret world of dreams, fantasies and the unconscious mind. Asariel is also the ruler of the Zodiac sign of Pisces — the Fishes. One characteristic of Pisceans is a dreamy, mystical nature often linked with latent psi abilities.

Developing Psychic Gifts

If you wish to develop your psychic awareness by means of magical candle burning, select a night when the moon is waxing and especially a day or two before the full moon. At this time the psychic currents are at their strongest and contact with the astral realms can be more easily achieved.

Position yourself in a well-ventilated room and if possible one with a window from which you can see the moon rising. Elaborate robes are not really that necessary. They impress nobody, least of all the Gods who have seen it all before! If you want to wear a robe, a simple black or white one in a kaftan design is the best. If you do not have a robe just dress sensibly and comfortably in normal clothes and make sure you have plenty of space to move around in.

Nine candles should be selected from your stock as this is a lunar number, representing the three phases of the moon (waxing, full and waning) multiplied by itself. Thirteen is another magical number associated with the lunar cycle as there are thirteen months or moons in a pagan's year. Because it was one of the mystic numbers used by practitioners of the Old Religion thirteen became somehow 'unlucky' or even 'evil'. Nine also occurs in many folk rituals and seasonal customs which is a direct reference to its ancient significance as a number associated with the worship of the moon goddess. Superstitions like these often survive in folk tradition because they relate to some half-forgotten aspect of the magical arts or pagan belief which has been misinterpreted by the popular mind.

The nine candles should be lit and at least one must be placed on a table in front of you. Behind it place a mirror to reflect the light. Sit quietly looking at the flame and breathing slowly to a regular rhythm. Counting one, two, three, in and four, five, six, seven, out is a good pattern to follow. After a while this breathing exercise will become second nature and you will not need to count the numbers mentally. This helps to calm the mind and can also be used for meditation purposes.

When you are completely calm and relaxed make the following invocation:

> Archangel Asariel, on this night as the moon
> rides high in the sky, draw aside the veil
> which hides the real from the unreal.
>
> Let me gaze beyond the portals of this world
> into the astral realms,
> Open my inner eye and let me look upon the
> unknown which is your secret land.

Move the single candle to one side and proceed to look into the mirror. After a few minutes of concentration changes may occur in it. The mirror's surface may cloud over or coloured lights will be seen floating in it. In some cases bright flashing lights can be seen or whirling patterns of energy. Eventually, with practice, symbols or images should appear in the mirror and these may have occult significance.

Never stare into the mirror for too long and resist the urge to lose yourself in the astral world. Remember Alice in Wonderland who went through the looking glass? Lewis Carroll knew something of 'secret things' and his charming fables for children conceal some gems of occult truth. Unfortunately, some who investigate the astral realm find it more exciting then the Earth plane and become 'prisoners in Fairyland'.

In any psychic work purple and/or silver candles can be used for they attract Otherworldly influences. The mirror technique described above can also be used for divination or predicting the future when the practitioner discerns omens and portents from the symbols or visions seen in the glass. For the best results scrying should be practised when the moon is in one of the water trinity of the Zodiac: Cancer, Pisces or Scorpio. In practical occultism water is a symbol of 'mind stuff' or the Astral Light, which is a carrier of vibrations and magical energy.

Candle magic and mirror magic can also be combined to read what occultists call the Akashic Records. The word *akasha* is an Eastern one meaning the essence of the Astral Light. By tuning into the Akashic Records the magus can discover, for instance, the details of past lives. The extent of the information which will be available from this source will depend on the personal development of the seeker. Usually he or she will only find out what is relevant to his or her present life and its karmic lessons. Research into past lives can be an absorbing occupation but it must never become and obsession. Morbid curiosity about past-life experiences is unhealthy and should be avoided.

A ritual for consulting the Akashic Records should be performed when the moon is in Capricorn (ruled by Saturn) and the invocation should be made to the Archangel Cassiel, Lord of Time and Karma. A black candle is burnt and the magus petitions the planetary angel of Saturn to reveal the information from the Akashic Records which is required. It may be that the magus is experiencing problems in his or her present life which are believed to be of karmic origin dating back to a previous experience and the Records can be consulted to try and solve the situation. After lighting the candle and invoking Cassiel the practitioner looks into the mirror and imagines a large old book whose pages are slowly turning. On these pages will be the words or pictures relating to the query. This type of ritual should never be practised light-heartedly, only with serious intent.

Some people, like Spiritualists, can accomplish the development of psi powers without the use of ritual accessories such as candles, mirrors or invocations to the Planetary Angels. Obviously their methods are just as valid, although they might take a little longer. By using ritual, and enlisting the assistance of the cosmic forces personified as gods or angels which rule the universe, the seeker is strengthening the efficacy of his or her willpower. Results can therefore be obtained more quickly and they will be more potent.

When a warrior rides out to do battle with the enemy in defence of truth and justice it is only sensible that he should use all the weapons in his armoury to achieve final victory. Similarly the wise person, the magus who is a spiritual warrior, will use all his or her gifts and knowledge to fulfil the desired aim and gain victory over life's capricious circumstances.

CHAPTER NINE

THE MYSTICAL NOVENA

It has been said that art imitates life, but it could also be said that religion imitates magic. In fact the magical arts are the older of the two, for in ancient times the celebrants of the official religion of any culture were also recognized as 'priest magicians'. Some aspects of this role were adopted by the priests of the Christian religion from the old pagan religions. In the early period of dual faith, churches often had twin altars, one dedicated to the new god and the other reserved for the old worship of the pagan deities. The priest may have taken the rite of communion each Sunday but on the full moon he also danced with the peasants in the woods celebrating the Old Ways. Even when Christianity finally outlawed pagan practices, it still owed a debt to their inspiration and influence. In this respect the Mass, with its powerful symbolism of sacrifice and transmutation, is a potent magical ritual when performed by someone who understands its occult significance.

Bearing this in mind we should not be surprised to learn that one of the most powerful rituals in candle magic is also practised by followers of the Roman Catholic Church. This devotion is called a 'novena', which the *Oxford English Dictionary* describes as 'special prayers or services enacted on nine successive days' (the lunar nine again!). Although today the novena is generally associated with

Christianity it had its origins in the magical rites of pagan times.

Concentrated effort is the key to any successful magical ritual which requires dedication, discipline and hard work. You will not get any worthwhile results if you just play at magic. This is illustrated graphically by the mystical novena for the practitioner has to be involved over a long period of time in a magical working involving invocations and ritual actions. This constant repetition of a ritual geared to a desired end result will eventually stir the Powers into action.

My occult teacher explained the *raison d'etre* of the novena to me by using the following simple allegory. She told me to imagine a builder equipped only with a small hammer who wants to demolish a high, thick wall. He knocks away steadily at the key points in the wall and as time passes, cracks begin to appear. These cracks widen and eventually the wall weakens and crashes down under the onslaught of the constant hammering. Magic worked through a novena operates on the same principle. Energy is generated over an extended period of time which works away at the obstacles preventing success. Eventually they weaken and are swept away by the flow of energy created by the concentrated effort over a length of time.

Vigils, intercessions and non-stop prayer sessions are a regular feature of religious devotion in nearly all the major world faiths. In Christian churches candles are lit to the saints and the Virgin Mary (the new version of the old pagan goddesses) and the faithful kneel in prayer for hours asking that their petitions be answered. In Buddhist temples a specially designed instrument known as a prayer wheel is used for intercessionary purposes. It consists of a hollow drum which revolves around a wooden shaft. In the personal version the drum is attached to a wooden ball on the end of a length of chain. Once it is set in motion by a spinning movement the whirling ball keeps the drum revolving with the slightest movement of the wrist. Inside the drum is a tightly wrapped roll of parchment on which are inscribed hundreds of prayers.

In the West the practising occultist, witch or magician replaces the saints either with the Planetary Angels or the pagan pantheon of gods of his or her choice. These can be Celtic, Norse, Egyptian, Babylonian, Hindu, Native American or whatever — it hardly matters which other than for personal and cultural considerations — for the angelic beings and the pagan gods are symbolic images of cosmic forces which have been clothed in archetypal forms. Many of the Christian saints are also pagan gods in disguise who were taken over when the early Church prohibited paganism.

We have seen above how the devout Roman Catholic prays to the saints but ignores the angels; this leads to an important omission which weakens the traditional power of the novena to produce results. According to ancient magical lore every hour of the day and night has an angelic ruler, whose planetary influence is stronger then than at other times. The individual rulerships of the hours are given below:

00.00 – 01.00 Sachiel
01.00 – 02.00 Anael
02.00 – 03.00 Uriel
03.00 – 04.00 Cassiel
04.00 – 05.00 Michael
05.00 – 06.00 Gabriel
06.00 – 07.00 Samuel
07.00 – 08.00 Raphael
08.00 – 09.00 Sachiel
09.00 – 10.00 Anael
10.00 – 11.00 Uriel
11.00 – 12.00 Cassiel
12.00 – 13.00 Michael
13.00 – 14.00 Gabriel
14.00 – 15.00 Samuel
15.00 – 16.00 Raphael
16.00 – 17.00 Sachiel
17.00 – 18.00 Anael
18.00 – 19.00 Uriel
19.00 – 20.00 Cassiel
20.00 – 21.00 Michael
21.00 – 22.00 Gabriel
22.00 – 23.00 Samuel
23.00 – 24.00 Raphael

Preparation for the Novena

When I was first taught the secrets of the mystical novena my occult teacher showed it to me as a turning wheel — The Wheel of Fortune as depicted in the Major Arcana of the Tarot cards — which carries along the magical vehicle which contains your desires. It is the wheel of The Chariot (another Tarot card) and this symbolizes the power of the will used as a battering ram by the mind to achieve any desired result. It is an energy sometimes associated with the angel Samuel and astrologically with the planetary force represented by the first Zodiac sign of Aries.

Each day is the first day of the rest of your life, but the day on which you light the first candle of your mystical novena is truly special. It is the day when you set in motion a magical juggernaut which will ultimately bring about what you desire. When you are working the novena you are not just invoking one of the Planetary Angels but the whole combined power force of the Angelic Hierarchy. It is their power which unleashes the minor forces sent to bring you the objective of this important magical ritual.

Before commencing the novena you must first ensure that you have a goodly supply of candles which are suitable for your purpose in the correct planetary colours. Night lights or votary candles are ideal but wicks floating in small bowls of oil are also useful. The bowls should be made of thick, heatproof glass and in different colours to represent the planets ruled by the Archangels.

Discovering your Ruling Angel

Before you are ready to begin the mystical novena you must first discover who your 'Ruling Angel' is. This is not your Guardian Angel, whom we shall encounter in a later chapter, but the Archangel who rules the Zodiac sign under which you were born. (Readers in doubt about their Ruling Angel should consult the information in chapters 3 and 4 relating to the Archangels, their planetary rulerships and the Zodiac signs in astrology.)

Having discovered who your Ruling Angel is you should begin the novena on his day and at the exact minute of his hour (as given in the list above) by lighting the first candle. The novena should end on his day and be finalized on the last minute of his hour on that day. When the first candle is lit your Ruling Angel should be addressed as follows:

O Archangel ... (*insert name*)
I light this sacred flame as
the first act of my petition
to the Angelic Hierarchy who
it is hoped will look with
favour on my request.

This mystical novena is
offered as a symbol of my
intent and with the hope
that my petition will be
answered.

As it is, so shall it be.

If you decide to work the novena use it to only petition for one wish. It is a magical ritual which is not designed for a multiplicity of requests, nor is it meant to deal with petty problems. The practice of the mystical novena should be the last resort and only used in emergencies when every other avenue has been explored and exhausted. Do not expect instant results; it takes time for the forces to do their work and sometimes it will take a full lunar cycle (approximately 28 days) for any results to be seen.

Working the Mystical Novena

During the actual novena the candles must be kept burning all the time if possible. Ideally the ritual should be performed over the magical period of nine days but this can be impractical. Alternatively, therefore, the novena can be worked over a 24-hour period. To illustrate how the novena actually operates in practice we will imagine that a student wishes to pass an important exam whose outcome will affect her future career prospects.

The student is a Leo whose astrological sign is ruled by the sun. Her Ruling Angel will therefore be the Archangel Michael and he will be invoked in the preliminary petition given above. For the 24-hour novena, the student lights the first orange or gold candle at 04.01 hours on a Sunday. At 07.01 hours she performs the following invocation to the Lord Raphael, who rules the matter under consideration, and lights a yellow candle:

> Archangel Raphael, Lord of Wisdom,
> I seek your help in time of need,
> Grant me the power of your quicksilver
> mind, your golden memory and your
> winged pen that I may successfully
> pass my exam on ... (*insert date*)
>
> Grant me Raphael, Lord of Books,
> intelligence and understanding
> that I may triumph over all
> odds and be successful.

When the next hour chimes the planetary rulership is transferred to the Archangel Sachiel and the student says:

> Archangel Sachiel, angel of the hour,
> assist me in my task and lend your
> power to my aim.

This process is repeated hourly through the day with each angel and at 15.00 and 23.00 hours the petition to Raphael is repeated. If you cannot face the thought of 24 hours without sleep, set an alarm clock during the night hours to wake you up when each invocation has to be made.

Remember that a candle must be kept burning all the time

throughout the mystical novena. Some magicians use seven candles or lights to represent the Planetary Angels or one votive candle is used in addition to the ones lit to invoke the Ruling Angel and the Archangel who governs the matter petitioned. However, the candles must be tended at all times and none should be allowed to go out during the ritual.

CHAPTER TEN

CONTACTING YOUR GUARDIAN ANGEL

Many aspects of candle magic, as we have seen, have their origins in ancient beliefs. Many of these date back thousands of years to when early humankind was in direct contact with the planetary gods or Archangels. This period is remembered in the collective unconscious of the human race as the so-called Golden Age when peace and harmony reigned on the Earth. In Judeo-Christian myth this stage in our evolution is represented by the legend of the Garden of Eden. The divine garden or earthly paradise is a myth common to all religious belief systems. Indeed many aspects of the story of Eden were borrowed by the Hebrews from the creation myths of the Babylonians and Sumerians.

This state of perfection, when the gods walked on the Earth, is believed by many occultists to have existed at the dawn of history when the earliest humans, referred to symbolically in the Biblical account as Adam and Eve, were ensouled with the divine spark of Godhead. During the primeval Golden Age it is said that humanity possessed telepathic powers, could speak the language of the animals, and was in contact with other realms of existence. This is illustrated in an allegorical form in the Biblical stories of God walking in the Garden of Eden and the intercourse between the so-called fallen angels and the daughters of men.

The Fall from Grace

According to ancient occult traditions, as humanity developed its first civilizations on the lost continents of Lemuria and Atlantis the esoteric knowledge possessed by its priesthood was misused. This is the reality behind the 'temptation' in the Garden of Eden when Adam and Eve ate the forbidden fruit of the Tree of the Knowledge of good and evil. Following this 'sin' the first couple were driven out of paradise by 'the angel with the flaming sword', who is sometimes identified as Samuel. A variation of this archetypal event is also found in the earliest shamanic beliefs where the Judeo-Christian fall from grace is known as The Great Separation which brought the Golden Age to a sudden end. Ever since, humanity has been striving to restore the Utopian state of innocence which one existed on Earth and is encapsulated in the myths of the religions of the world.

The same truth can be found in the myth of the war in heaven. In this allegory of Hebrew mythology, the Archangel Lumiel, who is the first born of creation, rebels against the divine plan. He is defeated in battle by the Archangel Michael and banished to assume the title *Rex Mundi* or Lord of the World. Previously Lumiel, or Lucifer, had been the solar angel and his place was taken by Michael. In the occult tradition the fall of Lumiel is seen as a supreme sacrifice enabling humanity to evolve. As the human race spiritually progresses so it can help the fallen archangel to regain his rightful place in creation.

It should be added here that such symbolic metaphors predate Christianity and the dualistic belief of Satanism, which is a Christian heresy. This dualism originated with the Manichean heresy which in turn was derived from the Persian religion of Zoroastrianism which believes that the universe is ruled jointly by the powers of darkness and the forces of light who are eternally struggling for supremacy. From such beliefs came the myth of the Devil, who was created by the early Church as a bogeyman to scare the medieval peasants into renouncing their pagan worship of the old Horned God of fertility.

It is following the Fall and the war in heaven that humankind as we know it was first fully incarnated into physical bodies on the material plane and developed the gender characteristics of male and female. At one stage in our evolution humans existed in a state of oneness with creation, and the next we had 'fallen' into gross materialism.

What have these ancient myths to do with candle magic and the concept of the Guardian Angel? They emphasize the fact that candle burning for occult purposes is one of the oldest occult arts practised by humanity. The myths also indicate that candle magic can be used by the dedicated student to re-establish lost communication with the spirit world and regain contact with the angelic realm.

Your Ruling Angel

Before explaining how to make a link with the Guardian Angel we will look more closely at the difference between it and the Ruling Angel who was described in the last chapter on the mystical novena.

As we know already, the Ruling Angel is found by looking up your Zodiac sign, finding its ruling planet, and then discovering which archangel is assigned to that planet. What does this mean in occult terms? Basically it means that all those born under a particular astrological sun sign are in sympathy with the vibration of their ruling planetary energy. This influence will figure strongly in the life patterns of all who share this birth sign. You can add extra power to the simple rituals of candle magic by invoking your Ruling Angel as we have seen working the novena.

The Ruling Angel can be called upon before embarking on any of the rituals of candle burning and a suggested wording is given below. In this example it is again presumed that the student has sun in Leo so the petition is addressed to the present solar angel, Michael.

> Mighty Archangel Michael, Lord of the Sun,
> I ... (*insert own name*) call upon you.

Assist me, Michael, in the Great Work and
grant a successful outcome to my efforts
through the power of the eternal light.

Your Guardian Angel

A Guardian Angel is far more personal than a Ruling Angel who, however much in tune with his vibration you may feel, is shared with all the other millions of people all over the world who were born in the same astrological month. A Guardian Angel is unique, and is regarded by many occultists as the higher self. In legend and folklore the Guardian Angel is said to attach itself to a baby at the moment of birth and remains as a protective spirit during that person's lifetime. Similarities between the Guardian Angel and the spirit guides who communicate with Spiritualist mediums have also been noted.

The belief in the existence of Guardian Angels is a very ancient one and is found in many religions and cultures worldwide. For instance, the pagan Romans believed in an entity known as the *genius* who not only protected its human companion from evil but also inspired him or her with the creative gifts of the Muses. In classical Greece the *genius* was known as a *daemon* (not to be confused with the Judeo-Christian demon or 'little devil') who was said to haunt writers, artists and poets and inspire them in their creative work.

The early Church naturally adopted the idea of Guardian Angels from these pagan originals. However, in dualistic fashion, they claimed that everyone had a bright angel of light who led them to righteousness and a dark angel who acted as a tempter. In Muslim belief we are protected by two angels in the day and two angels at night. These entities also record our deeds ready for the final reckoning on Judgement Day.

So much for the myths surrounding the Guardian Angel. How do you actually make contact with yours? The previous chapter on scrying described how to use a mirror to induce psychic vision. A mirror features again in the ritual for contacting the Guardian Angel, but in this case it is a special mirror manufactured specifically for communicating with your protecting angel, spirit guide or higher self.

Making the Magic Mirror

The magical mirror used for contacting the angelic forces should be made when the moon is waxing, on a Wednesday, and during one of the planetary hours ruled by the Archangel Raphael (Mercury). The reason for this is that the 'silvering' on mirrors, which gives them their reflective properties, is usually made from quicksilver or mercury. This is the sacred metal of the planetary sphere of Mercury which is ruled by the Lord Raphael.

The magical mirror can be manufactured from a round, concave piece of glass. A coat of matt black paint is used to cover the back of the glass (the convex side). Apply several layers fairly thickly but evenly over the whole surface. The finished mirror can then be mounted in a square of hardboard and placed in a strong picture frame. The surround can be painted and decorated to taste.

Consecrating the Mirror

Before the mirror is used it should be consecrated for the task ahead. This is done by placing three teaspoonsful of salt in a small bowl of fresh water (spring water is best but if not readily available tap water will suffice) and reciting the following:

> In the name of the Planetary Angels
> and the Great Spirit I ... (*insert
> name*) bless, purify and psychically
> cleanse this water for the task in
> preparation today.

As you say these words trace an imaginary pentagram or five-pointed star over the bowl of water with your hand. As you do this visualize the pentagram glowing with blue light which infuses the water. (This blessed water can be used for purifying purposes in the rite of exorcism previously described.)

Having completed the ritual of blessing the water take a virgin or brand-new cloth and wipe the face of the mirror with some of the water. Dry it with another new cloth and then discard both. Before using the mirror, leave it for the three nights leading up to the full moon in a position where it can reflect the lunar rays. The mirror is now 'charged' and ready for you to proceed to the actual magical operation of contacting your Guardian Angel.

Contacting Your Guardian Angel

Light a single white or silver candle in the place you have selected for the ritual, whether it be your temple, study or bedsitter. White is used for this working because it has a pure vibration which attracts higher forces. Silver is another colour associated with psychic forces and astral energies.

As you light the candle, say the following aloud:

> By the power of the Planetary Angels
> let this sacred place be protected
> from all negative thoughts and influences.
>
> Grant this day that the student of the
> Ancient Mysteries and the Great Magical
> Art standing here be allowed communion
> with his/her Guardian Angel,
> in the name of the Great Spirit,
> Cosmic Creator of the Universe.

Place the magical mirror in front of you on an altar, desk or table top so that you can look into it without strain. The electric light should have been switched off so that the room is only illuminated by the single candle. Look into the mirror as described in the previous chapter on psychic development. Breathe in and out slowly in a regular rhythm and look at yourself reflected in the mirror. If you can, look through and beyond the personal image you can see. You may see flickering, auric light composed of one or more colours dancing around your head. You may also feel aware of another presence or presences in the room. As soon as you feel tired cease working immediately for that day. Continue at a later time, or on another day, when you are completely refreshed.

After practice your efforts will eventually be rewarded. The image of yourself in the mirror may change or vanish completely to be replaced by the face of someone you do not know but who seems familiar. The lips of this person may move but you will hear the voice inside your mind. Sometimes the spirit guide or Guardian Angel will speak and the words will be heard aloud in the room. You can ask your new companion whatever questions you want, and two-way contact can be established between you and the spirit world.

Once communication is fully established with your Guardian Angel or spirit helper it may not always be necessary to use the mirror; however, firm ground rules should be laid down so that contact is made only when you desire it. It can be embarrassing if your guide suddenly wants to make contact at a crowded social gathering or in the middle of a rush-hour car journey!

When not in use the magical mirror should be wrapped in a cloth (not made from artificial material) and kept safely in a drawer or cupboard away from prying eyes and curious fingers. Do not allow the mirror to be exposed to sunlight as this neutralizes its powers. However it can be 'recharged' at any time by exposure to the rays of the full moon, which is the best time for contacting your Guardian Angel.

CHAPTER ELEVEN

CANDLES IN THE MAGICAL CIRCLE

Those readers who are familiar with any of the literature concerning the practice of magic in the Middle Ages will be aware of the importance of the magical circle in practical occult workings. Unfortunately the medieval magicians were often from a clerical background and had been heavily conditioned by Christian propaganda. The old grimoires or 'grammars' of magical theory and practice provide many lurid examples of the sensational aspects of the magical arts as they were practised in medieval times.

It is unfortunate that some of these superstitions were carried forward into the occult revival of the nineteenth century and we even find magicians then describing the magical circle in terms which were obviously negatively affected by the Church's bigoted ideas about the occult sciences. One classic example is the occultist Eliphas Levi, who had previously been a Catholic priest, who described a magical circle painted with a reversed cross in the centre and surrounded by the skull of a hanged criminal, the severed head of a black cat, the horns of a sacrificed goat and the corpse of a mummified bat!

Such horrific nonsense has no place in genuine magic or practical occultism; it is a prime example of how the magical arts were debased during the centuries of persecution. Because magicians and witches were forced underground by the Inquisition, all kinds of fanciful theories and misconceptions arose about their practices and beliefs. These were based on imagination in the absence of real information. Thankfully, the activities of responsible nineteenth-century groups like the Hermetic Order of the Golden Dawn and the modern occult and pagan revivalists has ensured that ritual magic, and the symbolism of the magical circle, has been restored to something resembling its original state.

In practice the magical circle has a twofold purpose: it acts as a psychic container for the energy produced during the ritual, and is also a clearly-defined 'sacred place' in which the magus can work and contact the Powers. Ideally it should be a separate room which should be reserved only for practical occult and psychic work, but this is seldom possible for most people. Therefore a ritual raising or construction of the magical circle every time you work will provide a temporary temple which can be physically dismantled after use. In occult lore the circle not only surrounds the magus in a two-dimensional sense but also exists three-dimensionally, extending above and below him or her to create a sphere of psychic protection and containment.

The Power of Light

What role do candles play in the magical circle? Early humans used fire to drive away wild animals and it therefore became a symbol of protection from danger. In ancient religious beliefs fire became a representation of the creative principle and an object of devout worship. The 'sacred flame' was regarded as a symbol of spiritual illumination or divine knowledge and the path of the hearth was followed by ordinary people who worshipped fire deities such as Brigid or Vestia. The sacred fire of the solar goddess Brigid at Kildare in Ireland was tended by nine virgin priestesses. With the coming of Christianity these priestesses became nuns who dedicated their lives to St Bridget and this practice survived into the twelfth century CE. The use of candles, torches and lamps in the magical circle derives from these early religious beliefs about the sacred nature of fire and their accompanying symbolism and magical rituals.

For instance in ancient times the shaman would dig a circular trench around his place of magical working. This was filled with brushwood and set alight. By making this ritual statement of intent in symbolic terms the shamans were creating a magical and psychic barrier between themselves and anyone who dared to disturb the ritual. The shaman was also deliberately setting aside a sacred ground, a 'place between the worlds', where spiritual forces could be invoked and magical energies weaved. The symbolism of weaving magic was a powerful metaphor in shamanism and the occult practices which later derived from it. It is found especially in traditional witchcraft where the recognition sign between members of the sisterhood is a spindle, representing the Triple Goddess who weaves the web of fate and destiny which binds humanity to the material plane.

The Archangels of the Elements

Except in the circumstances involving protection from psychic attack, the casting of the magical circle involves the use of four candles. These are placed at the quarters or compass points to represent the Archangels of the Elements. They are Michael (fire) assigned to the south whose colour is gold or orange, Gabriel (water) ruling the west whose colour is blue, Uriel (earth) ruling the northern quarter whose colour is brown or black, and Raphael (air) guarding the east quarter whose colour is yellow.

Descriptions of the magical images of Michael, Gabriel and Raphael have already been provided. Uriel is the planetary ruler of the far-flung sphere of Uranus which was only discovered in the eighteenth century, although its astrological and magical influence had been known since ancient times. In archetypal imagery the Uranian angel is visualized as a stern-faced man of mature age. He has long, flowing, silver hair and violet eyes and wears a cloak of flashing, rainbow hues. On his forehead is the 'television aerial' symbol of the planet Uranus as depicted in astrology.

Each of the Archangels of the Elements is accompanied by his personal *magitellus* or elemental server in the form of one of the Kings or Lords of the elemental forces. (Although traditionally masculine titles are used for these entities they are in fact asexual.) These spirits of the elements are known as the Mighty Ones in modern Wicca and the Lords of the Watchtowers in ceremonial magic.

They are Djinn, Lord of the Salamanders (fire spirits), Niksa, Lord of the Undines (water spirits), Ghob, Lord of the Gnomes (earth spirits) and Paralda, Lord of the Sylphs (air spirits). These elemental spirits were first named by the medieval occultist Paracelsus who derived their descriptive names from classical sources. Salamander comes from Salambe meaning 'fire place', gnome is from gnoma meaning 'knowledge', sipha means 'butterfly' and undine originates from unda or 'wave'.

In Egyptian magic the elemental rulers are represented by the four children of the falcon-headed solar god Horus, who is the son of Osiris and Isis. They are known as Toumantph, the jackal guardian of fire; Kabexnuf, the hawk lord of water; Alephi, the ape guardian of earth, and Ameshut, the human ruler of air. Another representation of the rulers of the elemental forces can be found in the Minor Arcana of the Tarot where they are the Kings and Queens of Swords (fire), Cups (water), Pentacles (earth), and Wands (air).

Djinn's archetypal form has already been described and the others can be visualized in their traditional humanoid forms as follows:

Niksa as ruler of the watery element is fluid and ever changing. His greenish-blue aura is splashed with silver and grey streaks of light.

Ghob is Lord of the Earth element and is a squat and heavy in shape. He can be visualized as a traditional gnome or goblin exuding a timeless aura of power and wisdom.

Paralda is a lithe, writhing figure composed of pale blue and grey mist. His form is tenuous and indistinct and, like Niksa, he is constantly changing shape.

These descriptions of the elemental guardians of the magical circle are archetypal or telesmatic images visualized by the magus to contact the relevant spirit force they represent. They are purely imaginative forms but will appear in this shape to the psychic vision of a seer or clairvoyant and they should be imagined in this symbolic form by the magician.

Each of the elements has a symbolic meaning and, in accordance with the ancient Hermetic axiom 'As above, so below', the elemental forces not only exist in the physical world of Nature but are also reflected in the inner world of human nature. A short description of each of the elements and their attributes is given below.

Fire represents energy and force. It has rulership over healing, creativity, purification, destruction and sexual energy. It symbolizes the willpower of the magus which is channelled through ritual to produce changes in his or her personality or environment.

Water is the elemental principle of movement and change. It has rulership over the imagination, the emotions, inspiration, dreams, psychic awareness, and love.

Earth is a symbol of endurance and stability. It also symbolizes Nature, fertility, growth, death and regeneration.

Air represents adaptability and expansion. It has rulership over memory, communication, intelligence, visualization and concentration.

Casting the Circle

It is not always necessary to cast a magical circle for occult workings but should you want to do so then the following information may be useful.

Circle casting usually begins either in the east or the north. In the occult tradition and the pagan Mysteries the north is regarded as a sacred direction and the home of the oldest gods. This is because of the ancient beliefs and myths relating to the North or Pole Star, which in shamanism was regarded as the *axis mundi* or centre of the universe. The east is traditionally (if not actually) the direction in which the sun rises each morning at dawn. In esoteric tradition the solar orb is a symbol of the creative life force which permeates and sustains the universe. This is why the circle is usually drawn (actually or in the imagination of the practitioner) in a deosil or sunways direction, i.e. clockwise. There are, however, instances when the circle is drawn widdershins, or anti-clockwise, such as when the practitioner is banishing negative conditions or unwanted influences and when the circle is closed after a ritual.

The circle can be drawn with a specially-prepared wand or staff or by using your finger and the power of the imagination, which is the most potent magical tool of all. Whichever method you use on the physical plane the circle must always be created on the mental and astral levels as well. This is done by imagining a ring of blue light or flames leaping up where your hand or magical instrument is pointing. This technique is similar to the creation of the circle of psychic self-protection mentioned earlier.

To add extra power and protection to the magical circle you can then invoke or call upon the Archangels of the Elements and their attendant elemental guardians. This is done in turn beginning with Raphael in the eastern quarter and moving clockwise around the circle invoking each angel at his relevant compass point as follows:

> Archangel Raphael/Michael/Gabriel/Uriel
> I ask you to protect and guard this circle
> from all negative forces and thoughts and
> show favour to the magical work performed
> within it.

As you call upon the Archangels of the Elements visualize them standing around the circle in their archetypal forms. To evoke or summon forth the elemental guardians of the magical circle you should repeat the following words at each of the quarters, again beginning at the east:

> O Paralda/Djinn/Niksa/Ghob
> spirit of the east/south/west/north,
> I evoke your presence to protect
> the circle during my workings.

It is of course foolish to think that the practitioner, as a mere mortal, is actually commanding the great cosmic forces personified by the angelic beings to attend his or her circle personally. What is in fact happening is that the invocation of the Planetary Angels, together with the visualization of their archetypal images, is tuning the magus into the *power* represented by these aspects of the Cosmic Creator. This is the process which occurs every time we invoke the Angelic Hierarchy during the rituals of candle burning.

Closing the Circle

When you have completed your candle magic (or any other type of occult or psychic work) within the the circle it is then closed down. Again, starting from the eastern quarter, go round the circle repeating the following words at each of the compass points:

> Archangel Raphael/Michael/Gabriel/Uriel
> I thank you for your help in my magical
> endeavours and your protection of the
> circle during the Great Work.

To dismiss the elemental guardians the following words are recited at each of the quarters, beginning at the east:

> O Paralda/Djinn/Niksa/Ghob,
> spirit of the east/south/west/north,
> I thank you for your attendance

during this ritual and hereby dismiss
you from the circle.

The four candles in the circle are then extinguished and the magical images of the Archangels of the Elements and the elemental guardians are visualized fading away. As stated earlier, the circle can be closed by walking around it in an anti-clockwise direction. Some practitioners even reverse the sequence of the angelic and elemental dismissals. After you have closed the circle it is often a good idea to 'earth' yourself by having a meal, especially if you have not eaten for some time before the ritual. Lovemaking is another nice way to release the tension that often builds up during magical of psychic work.

This, then, is the real magical circle. No human skulls, cats' heads, goat horns or any of the other weird paraphernalia featured in horror videos or occult thrillers. In common with all genuine forms of magical practice it is simple, straightforward and harmless.

CHAPTER TWELVE

GENERAL RITUALS AND CANDLE DIVINATION

In this chapter I would like to provide the apprentice candle-burner with a selection of additional rituals which can be used for various purposes. These do not fit into any particular category and deserve a special mention in this separate section.

The Dream Wish Ritual

In our introduction to candle magic the importance of the subconscious mind was stressed together with its receptiveness to visual images. These characteristics are brought together and employed directly to produce results in the Dream Wish Ritual. It is designed to work a clever magical trick with the power of the unconscious which involves a projected thought form.

First, select a candle from the range you keep exclusively for use in magic. Depending on the object of the wish a candle of the corresponding astral colour should be chosen. Gently handle the candle so that you become attuned to its special colour vibration. As with the oiling preparation, do this with care so it does not break nor does the wax melt in the warmth of your hand. As you handle it see in your mind's eye the nature of your wish and exactly what you want the end result of the ritual to be.

Having done this, place the candle in a corner of your bedroom so it is directly opposite your place of rest. Light the candle an hour before you usually go to bed so that you have ample time to perform the ritual. As you light the candle say:

> Archangel Uriel, Planetary Angel of Uranus,
> I ask for your help and inspiration this night.
> As I sleep weave your magical web, grant the
> innermost wish that is in my heart now.

Having said your invocation to Uriel the wish must be then expressed in a more concrete form in order to bring it into manifestation. This will require a clean piece of paper (virgin parchment, or the skin of a black lamb sacrificed at the dark of the moon, is not required as this is a modern magical grimoire!). The paper should be blank and with a pencil, crayon or felt-tipped pen draw a simple picture of your objective.

Naturally this does not have to be an expert work of art for in magical working the intention and dedication is more important than artistic talent which is good news for those of us who did not manage 'O' level art. It is the thought *behind* the picture which is important. In the Dream Wish Ritual you are using a visual image to liberate the powers of the subconscious and bring into manifestation whatever you desire through the enactment of the ritual.

As an example, let us say that you are thinking of moving house and want to find a suitable new home. On the piece of paper you should draw a picture of your ideal home — just the outline will do, with perhaps the number of windows, the front door and the garden gate. Alternatively you may wish to cut out a magazine illustration and use that or, if there is a specific house in question, use the photograph from the estate agent's brochure.

89

When the picture is ready you should call upon Uriel for help once more as follows:

> Archangel Uriel, planetary ruler of Uranus,
> spin the wheel of fortune and grant me my
> wish this night.

Sit quietly for a few minutes meditating on the image of the wish that you have created. Then take the piece of paper and carefully fold it into three. Place the folded paper under your pillow before you go to bed. Leave the candle to burn down during the hours of darkness, ensuring that it is safe. In the morning remove the paper from its resting place and say the following:

> Archangel Uriel, Lord of Uranus,
> I thank you for your help in this
> matter and by your power may my
> dreams come true.

The folded paper is then burnt in the candle flame and the ashes disposed of safely.

During the night the visual image you have created has entered your subconscious mind and your angelic invocation has started to shape forces on the inner planes which will manifest your desire in the physical world.

Uriel is the angel of the unexpected, the sudden change of circumstances or unsuspected strokes of luck. As he rules electricity he is the archangel who produces the 'bolt from the blue' that can transform circumstances, get stagnant conditions moving again or change life for the better. He is therefore the ideal patron for this type of ritual.

Do not necessarily expect a phone call next morning from the estate agent offering some inflated sum for your semi-detached so you can buy a country mansion with 200 acres. Nor should you expect to win a fortune on the football pools or meet the lover of your dreams in the local supermarket. As with all acts of candle magic, your goals have to be realistic but you may always be pleasantly surprised by the results of your workings.

Astral Travelling

A variation on the Dream Wish Ritual can also be used for astral travelling, which today is often called, in quasi-scientific terms, 'out of the body experiences'. In occult belief your body has an astral or etheric counterpart which can vacate the physical form and travel, at the speed of light, anywhere on the planet or into other dimensions and the spirit world. This astral double is attached to the physical body by a 'silver cord' so it can return at any time. This psychic umbilical cord is only broken at the moment of death when the soul leaves its physical vehicle and passes to the Otherworld.

Again, you should light your candle as described in the Dream Wish spell. However, this time you should use a silver candle and invoke the Archangel Asariel, the planetary angel of Neptune. In occult lore and myth Asariel has rulership over psychic powers and the astral plane. He should be invoked as follows:

Lord Asariel, ruler of the starry astral
realms, show me in my dreams the place I
wish to visit.

Write on a piece of clean, blank paper the name of the place or person you wish to visit astrally. Fold it into three and place the paper under your pillow before you go to bed. During the night you will visit the place you have nominated. If you wish to project your astral body to visit a specific person, do remember that his or her privacy should be respected and you should resist any temptation to become an astral 'peeping tom'.

Divining the Future

Candle magic can be used to foretell the future by means of the creation of a *magistellus* or familiar spirit. In the Middle Ages no self-respecting witch or wizard was without a familiar, one of whose magical uses was in divination. To create your own *magistellus*, select a new candle from your stock. For this magical operation a plain white one is probably best. Prepare it by the dressing procedure and then say:

> Creature of the candle in the name of
> the Planetary Angels I conjure you to
> be my magistellus.
>
> Candle of light, creature of the fire,
> I instruct you to show me the secrets
> of past, present and future.

Light the candle and place it on your altar, desk or table top. Stare intently at the candle flame and you will notice it rise and fall, growing larger and smaller. Initially you can place your hand, positioned safely some inches above the candle, to draw the flame up and down. It will respond to the auric emanations of your skin extending from the palm and fingers.

After a little practice you will find you can command the candle flame to rise and fall at will. You have therefore proved your mastery over the fire geni or spirit which inhabits the flame. Once this has been achieved you can use your familiar as an oracle to give advice on problems and situations. This is accomplished by means of a simple question and answer system using the increase in the flame for a 'yes' and a decrease as a 'no'. It is essential when consulting the fire oracle that you keep your mind as empty of thoughts as possible. In contrast to the first exercise above, do not deliberately attempt to affect the movement of the candle flame with the power of the mind.

Weather Magic

In olden times the practice of natural magic (to which candle burning belongs) often involved the magical influencing of the weather. Witches were often credited with raising storms and sailors used to buy special charms made from knotted cords from the local wisewoman. These knots were untied at sea to conjure up a wind in the days of the great sailing ships. Candle magic can be used to change the weather as in the following simple ritual.

On a cloudy day place a new gold or orange candle on the windowsill. (Make sure it is safely away from the curtains!) Light the candle, saying:

> Lord Lumiel, Angel of the Morning and
> the Golden Dawn, hear my petition,
> as this light shines below sweep aside
> the grey clouds and let the Sun above
> shine down on the earth.

After saying these words, meditate on the candle flame and imagine the clouds parting, patches of blue sky appearing and then the sun's rays shining down on the landscape outside the window. Do this until the candle burns down.

With the future threat of global warming it may be that the requirement will be for rain rather than sunshine. In that case candle magic can be used to invoke one of the 'watery' angels, such as Gabriel or Asariel.

Healing the Earth

Generally, occult tradition, the magical arts and the pagan religions have always been 'environmentally friendly'. The ancients worshipped Nature as a manifestation of the divine, regarded the Earth as sacred, and celebrated the changing seasons with religious festivals. Today many occultists, Wiccans and neo-pagans are actively involved with environmental protection groups like Greenpeace and Friends of the Earth and many perform magical rituals to preserve the natural world. The following candle magic ritual can be used for that purpose.

Ideally the ritual should be performed in an outdoor setting.

While the practitioner need not go skyclad, he or she can work in bare feet so direct contact is made with the earth energies. Five candles are needed for this ritual and they should be coloured yellow, orange/gold, blue and black/brown (to represent the four elemental quarters) and green (symbolizing Mother Earth and the planetary angel of Venus, Anael). As this is an alfresco working the candles should be placed in suitable containers so they are not extinguished by the breeze.

The four Angels of the Elements and the elemental guardians should be invited to attend the ritual as described in the procedure for casting the magical circle. The green candle is then lit and the following invocation is made:

> Archangel Anael, Lord of Venus,
> I/we invoke your help to heal
> and cleanse Mother Earth in
> the name of the Great Spirit

Then at each of the compass points the Planetary Angels representing each of the elemental forces should be invoked in turn as follows:

East Archangel Raphael, Lord of Mercury,
ruler of the air and the winds,
I/we invoke you to heal and purify
Mother Earth and cleanse her atmosphere.

South Archangel Michael, Lord of the Sun,
ruler of fire and flame, I/we invoke
you to heal and purify Mother Earth
and cleanse her energy sources.

West Archangel Gabriel, Lord of the Moon,
ruler of the waters, I/we invoke you
to heal and purify Mother Earth and
cleanse her oceans.

North Archangel Uriel, Lord of Uranus,
ruler of the elemental forces of

earth, I/we invoke your help to
heal and purify Mother Earth and
cleanse her soil.

Sit in the centre of the circle and meditate on the image of Earth as seen from outer space. Visualize the planet surrounded by a halo of blue light and see its atmosphere purified of pollution, its oceans cleared of sewage and radioactive waste and its earth cleansed of chemical fertilizers and toxins. When the meditation has been completed the magical circle can be closed in the traditional manner.

As with all the rituals in this book, the practitioner can substitute the details of the angelic forces mentioned above for the corresponding archetypes from their own religious pantheon. However, one word of warning, it is not advisable to mix god forms from different cultures or pantheons in the same ritual. This can cause severe spiritual indigestion!

CHAPTER THIRTEEN

INCENSE MAGIC

During the centuries the burning of incense for magical purposes has been closely linked with candle magic. In an earlier chapter we saw how candles could be impregnated with perfume or incense grains to produce evocative odours. In the lore of magical correspondences, which tunes the magus to the natural forces controlling the universe, incenses can be used to contact a specific planetary energy. They can also be used to produce a certain state of mind or atmosphere conducive to magical work.

In ancient times incense was widely used in a religious context for several reasons. Firstly, it was burnt to create a pleasing aroma that it was believed would attract the Gods. Its second use was to mask the offensive odours of blood sacrifice and to purify the atmosphere during the funeral rites for the dead. As humanity developed and the cruel practice of sacrifice was prohibited the incense itself became a harmless substitute for the sacrificial offerings. Lastly, incense was used when prayers were offered because it was believed the petitions of the worshippers would be carried up to heaven on the spirals of sweet smoke.

Historically, incense was extensively used for religious ritual among all the ancient peoples, including the Hebrews. In the Bible can be found the divine commandment 'And thou shalt make an altar to burn incense upon' and 'Aaron shalt burn thereon sweet incense every morning' (Exodus 30, 1 and 7). The Hebrews also used incense for domestic purposes to purify their bedchambers and clothes. It is almost certain that the children of Israel adopted the use of incense from their pagan neighbours who included the Sumerians, Babylonians, Chaldeans, Canaanites and Egyptians.

The Ancient Egyptians in particular were masters of incense burning. It was said when a wise person died in Egypt his or her soul was carried to the Halls of Amenti, the abode of the Gods, on the swirling clouds of smoke from the temple censers. Outside the practice of religious rites the Egyptian physicians used incense to cleanse and purify the sickrooms of their patients. They also combined its use with aromatic perfumes derived from the essential oils extracted from plants. These were massaged into the body of the sick person and this magical ritual formed the historical origin for the modern New Age practice of aromatherapy.

In Ancient Egypt the compounding of the herbs, flower extracts, gums and essential oils used to make incense was a task considered so important that it was restricted to only a few specially-trained priests. During the manufacturing process magical words of power were chanted and after its preparation the incense was sealed in clay containers. This was to protect it from the severe desert heat and also prevent its theft by those who wanted to use it for magical purposes. Anyone who stole the recipes from the temple incense faced the death penalty and his family were ritually cursed by the priests. So potent were the incenses formulated by the Egyptians that when the 1922 expedition led by Howard Carter and Lord Caernarvon broke into the tomb of the boy king Tutankhamun they discovered that the subtle fragrance of the incense burnt during his burial rites still lingered in the air.

Centuries ago incense and anointing oils were often employed outside of religious ceremonies and magical rites for social reasons although their occult properties were still recognized. As the ingredients for making incense were often very expensive and often had to be imported into the country of use the burning of incense became a status symbol among the wealthy. Throughout the ages courtesans and queens have used incense and exotic oils for sexual attraction. It is alleged that Cleopatra, who was a priestess of Isis and well versed in the occult arts, enslaved her male lovers by her skilful knowledge of rare incenses and oils which she burnt in silver dishes in her royal apartments. It was said that the queen soaked her gowns in a specially-prepared musky perfume which drove men mad with desire.

In the Middle Ages incense was used by magicians when conjuring up spirits. It was believed that an elemental spirit could use the incense smoke to build up its form. It then materialized in the 'triangle of art' drawn by the magus outside his magical circle for this purpose. Unfortunately some of the ingredients of these medieval incenses often owed more to the imagination of the practitioner than to good censing! One grimoire of medieval magic describes an incense which allegedly assisted the magician to call up the spirits of the moon. It was made of the crushed root of a mandrake (the English white bryony) which must be torn from the ground by a dog on the night of the full moon, dried flowers of convolvulus, the seeds of a poppy plant and a pinch of sulphur. This mixture was ground up and made into a paste, using the blood of a black cat, and then burnt.

Here we can see the law of magical correspondences at work but due to popular ignorance of the occult principles behind magic they have become debased. Bryony, convolvulus and poppy are all flowers sacred to the moon goddesses worshipped in pagan times. It was believed that mandrakes screamed when they were pulled out of the ground, hence the use of an animal to do the deed for it was believed anyone who heard the noise would go mad. In fact, because of their deep roots, mandrakes do make a squeaking noise when they are pulled up and popular superstition created the rest of the folk tale. The addition of sulphur and cat's blood (even if cats are often regarded by superstitious folk as creatures of the moon) adds the unnecessary element of sensationalism which unfortunately characterizes so much of medieval magic.

Modern Uses of Incense

Students of the magical arts today can use incense either for relaxation purposes during meditation or to contact the archetypal energies represented by the Planetary Angels or pagan gods. The creation of the scents used in magical rituals can be achieved by using a variety of mediums. Probably the simplest method is to release the scent of specific flowers which are sacred to the divine forces by crushing their leaves. Essential oils can also be extracted from plants and used as perfumes or for anointing. Alternatively, the dried foliage of herbs and flowers are burnt to create an aromatic effect. Various types of blended incense can be purchased nowadays from occult suppliers, although these tend to be offered for sale in small quantities at high prices. For a general incense a good quality product can be obtained from church suppliers. One example is the famous range of incenses produced by the Benedictine monks of Prinknash Abbey in Gloucestershire.

Some practising occultists blend their own incenses, which is a relatively cheap and also interesting hobby. The situation has changed dramatically since I first began to study the magical arts. With the advent of the 'hippies' in the sixties and seventies and the present New Age interest in aromatherapy a wide range of natural essential oils are now available in High Street shops. Herbs can also be purchased from wholefood outlets or a wide range of seeds can be obtained if you want to grow your own.

Manufactured incenses come in two main forms: grains (powder) or joss sticks. There are obvious advantages to the use of the latter as they are readily available and simple to use. Unfortunately the setback is that the range of fragrances which are on offer can be limited due to their Eastern origin. For the beginner, however, they often provide an ideal way of burning incense at a low cost and for this reason can be recommended.

Incenses in grain form are slightly more difficult to use and you will require some equipment. Again church suppliers (and some occult shops) will be able to offer professional censers as used in churches. A word of caution is needed here as they can be awkward for the inexperienced to handle. The resulting tangled chains could lead to a burnt carpet or personal injury if employed in a confined space. In solitary workings, which this book is designed for, the effort and discipline required to swing a censer can also be a serious obstacle to concentration.

This is why I would recommend the use of a suitable, static alternative, which can be made quite simply by half filling a small pottery bowl with sand. This makes a very good censer and will only cost a few pence. Incense can be burnt safely in this either by sprinkling grains onto a self-igniting charcoal block or by placing joss sticks directly into the sand. The metal foil containers in which frozen foods are sometimes sold can be used as makeshift incense burners. Perforated to allow air intake, they can turned upside down and the charcoal block placed on top. Alternatively, small holes can be made in the reversed container in which incense sticks can be placed.

Magical Censing

As we know from modern scientific research, smell is a very important aspect of the human sensing mechanism. For instance the natural odours of the body play an essential role in the chemical reactions which cause sexual attraction between men and women. Different smells, whether pleasant or not, can act as mental stimulants and trigger visual images in the mind conjuring up nostalgic memories of the past. On a psychic and magical level, differing aromatics are capable of producing degrees of vibration in the atmosphere. Occultists are of the opinion that these attract specific influences or cause changes in consciousness, which are the primary objectives of any magical ritual.

Each of the astrological signs and planets has its own associated individual herbs, flowers and aromatics in the lore of magical correspondences. A study of these will indicate to the aspiring magus the correct incense or essential oil which can be formulated for a ritual invoking these energies. Details of these correspondences are given below using the planetary rulership as the prime indicator.

Sun
Astrologically the sun rules the Zodiac sign of Leo and its planetary rulership is under the influence of the Archangel Michael. The flowers and herbs which are associated with the solar orb are sunflower, marigold, heliotrope, saffron and rosemary. Traditionally the incense used for magical workings to contact the solar energies is frankincense.

Moon
In astrology the moon rules Cancer and is under the angelic rulership of Gabriel. The following flowers and herbs are assigned to the lunar sphere of influence: convolvulus, poppy, camphor, patchouli, narcissi, madonna lilies and jasmine. As can be seen from this list, the perfumes associated with the moon are of the heavy type which cause drowsiness or, as in the case of the opium poppy, have narcotic effects. This ties in with the magical correspondence of the lunar sphere as linked with psychic matters, dreams and intuition.

Mercury
According to the classical system Mercury rules Virgo and Gemini and is under the rulership of the Archangel Raphael. Incenses for the invocation of this planetary energy should be composed from sandalwood, mint, cloves, cinnamon, verbena, marjoram or lemon leaves. These are mostly perfumes with a sharp, pungent smell, capable of stimulating the mind.

Venus
Astrologically, this planet rules the Zodiac signs of Taurus and Libra which provide the contrasting aspects of the Venusian energy which is reflected in the list of correspondences. Venus is governed by the Archangel Anael.

The list of plants and aromatics sacred to the planet of love include ambergris, musk, vervain, violet, bergamot and rosewood.

Some of these are associated with the sexual aspect of Venus while others are softer and more fragrant indicating a more romantic form of love.

Mars
The red planet in the solar system rules Aries and Scorpio and its archangel is Samuel, who in Hebrew mythology was the consort of the owl goddess Lilith of the dark moon.

The herbs and plants which come under Martian rulership include pine, garlic, cumin, ginger, paprika and hawthorn blossom. These aromatics are of a 'hot', spicy or astringent type which stimulates the senses.

Jupiter
Astrologically this planet rules Sagittarius and Pisces and is governed by the Archangel Sachiel. The correspondences for the Jovian sphere of influence are borage, lilac, magnolia and sage. All these have an odour which could be described as 'expansive', indicating the influence of Jupiter in both magic and astrology.

Saturn
In the Zodiac the dark planet rules Capricorn and Aquarius and is governed by the time Lord Cassiel. The aromatics associated with Saturn are myrrh, henbane and yew which emphasize the death aspect of this planetary energy. Incenses of this type would be suitable for the rites of the departed.

In common with candle burning, the use of incense in magical rituals is based on the most important element known to humanity — fire. By employing incense in his or her workings the magical practitioner is demonstrating mastery over that elemental force which has played a central role in religious belief and daily life since ancient times. Candle and incense magic can be seen as one of the most natural of the magical arts and as such are ideal for those stepping on to the occult path for the first time.

CHAPTER FOURTEEN

PRACTICAL CONCLUSIONS

As I stated in Chapter 1 the use of the angelic images throughout this book is deliberate. The concept of angels is one that most people can relate to as they have been familiar with it since childhood. This book was written for beginners and so most readers will be newcomers to the occult path and practical magic. I hope they will find the concept of the Angelic Hierarchy an easy one to understand and work with in their candle burning.

Those of you who may be more experienced in these matters, especially those following non-Christian belief systems (and in our multi-cultural society their number is increasing steadily despite harassment from the media and fundamentalists), can substitute names and images from your own divine pantheon. However, you should not reject the validity of the angels for they originated with the old planetary gods of the Middle Eastern pagan religions. Ultimately it matters little what names we use, except for cultural reasons for, as the famous occultist Dion Fortune so wisely said, 'All the Gods are one God'.

Eight Basic Rules

I hope that the main points of candle burning for magical purposes have been fully understood by the reader but the basic rules have been summed up below:

1 Candles and incense are used to create 'magical' effects because candlelight and the smell of perfume can cause changes in normal patterns of perception, mental understanding and emotional reaction. They also provide a focus for concentration and have the power to attract influences from the astral and spiritual planes of existence. Candle and incense burning provides the sensory framework within which the mind of the magus can enter a receptive state so that contact can be made with extra-physical forces. While these are represented on the mental level by archetypal images in the imagination of the practitioner, the would-be magician should be under no illusion that these forces do exist in reality.

2 Different colours have different vibrations and oscillate psychically on various levels. Each colour attracts a specific influence which has both a spiritual and psychological meaning. The candle burner should be careful to select the correct colour for his or her purpose using the guide in this book.

3 A candle can be used to represent a third person in a ritual by using one whose astrological colour relates to his or her birth sign. This is particularly useful in healing rituals for instance.

4 Candles employed for magic should never be used again, especially for domestic purposes, but allowed to burn down. In every case virgin or new materials should be used. If possible make your own candles but if they have to be purchased from a shop do not haggle over the price and give the exact money for them.

5 Always 'dress' or oil the candles before use. This simple act is important as it 'charges' or magnetizes them with your personal vibrations.

6 Never ever be tempted to use candle magic to influence people against their will, to bring harm to others or for any destructive, anti-social or immoral purpose. Remember, if misused, magical power and psychic energy has a 'fail safe' and can return threefold to the sender which is not a very pleasant experience.

7 Take notice of the cosmic tides and flow with them. Work with these tides whenever possible, not against them. A few simple rules are that you attract on the waxing moon, work psychically at full moon, banish on the waning moon and start new projects at new moon. Unless you feel an affinity with Lilith, or any other aspect of the Dark Goddess, avoid working any magic on the dark of the moon (three days before new moon).

8 Always be extra careful when using either candles or incense, especially in a confined space. Fire is a powerful and dangerous element, more so when you are dealing with it magically, and should be treated with due respect. Safety precautions should be a priority at all times to protect yourself and others. Ideally it is a good idea to have some method of extinguishing a fire close at hand.

These eight rules are fundamental to candle and incense burning and should be followed at all times. Providing the practitioner has a degre of self-discipline and is willing to work hard to attain results he or she will be successful. Although the material provided in this book is designed for use by beginners, once students become more experienced they can experiment with their own variations using the basic outlines provided. In practical magic there are no stone tablets engraved in fire and dogma is a dirty word to most magicians.

Always remember that, as in life, what you get of magic will depend to a large extent on your level of commitment what you actually put into it. People who know very little about real magic (although they will often refer to themselves to adepts — a sure sign that they are no such thing!) seem to believe that dressing up in elaborate costumes, buying expensive magical equipment, performing theatrical rituals and claiming initiation into some mysterious centuries old secret society is what is is all about. Others believe that all you have to do is mumble 'words of power' in a foreign language (usually a long dead one), wear a 'power crystal' and wave a magical sword around and miracles will happen.

You may well be a seven-degree Grand Wombat with a 10 inch wand but you are also living in a fantasy world. Both these approaches only reveal the ignorance of those 'magicians' who expound them to the general public. It is not an attitude which is found among genuine practitioners of the magical arts and is not endorsed within the pages of this book.

The practice of magic is hard work yet it is also, paradoxically, simplicity itself. Only by working in harmony with the powers of Fate can you ever hope to be master or mistress of your own destiny. The simple arts of incense and candle magic are the first step on that long road and can be seen as a stepping-stone to higher attainments on the spiritual path.

MAGICAL CORRESPONDENCES

Sun

Planetary influence	Rules success, ambition, career, physical healing, personal finance, officialdom and sport
Day of the week	Sunday
Archangel	Michael
God forms	Apollo, Brigid, Helios, Lugh, Ra, Sekhmet
Zodiac sign	Leo
Element	Fire
Planetary colour	Gold/orange
Planetary metal	Gold
Incense	Frankincense
Flowers	Marigold, heliotrope, sunflower
Animal	Wild cat
Bird	Hawk

Moon

Planetary influence	Rules psychic powers, the home, dreams, childbirth, women, travel by sea

Day of the week	Monday
Archangel	Gabriel
God forms	Artemis, Diana, Hathor, Hecate, Selene, Sin
Zodiac sign	Cancer
Element	Water
Planetary colour	Silver/blue
Planetary metal	Silver
Incense	Jasmine
Flowers	Night-scented stock, convolvulus, poppy
Animals	Crab
Birds	Owl, nightjar

Mercury

Planetary influence	Rules communication, memory, education, mental healing, travel, commerce, writing, acting, finding lost or stolen property
Day of the week	Wednesday
Archangel	Raphael
God forms	Athene, Hermes, Mercury, Odin, Ogma, Thoth
Zodiac signs	Gemini and Virgo
Element	Air
Planetary colour	Yellow
Planetary metal	Quicksilver
Incense	Sandalwood
Flowers	Fern, broom, fennel
Animal	Dog
Bird	Magpie

Venus

Planetary influence	Rules romantic love, beauty, marital affairs, music, the environment, fashion and the arts

Day of the week	Friday
God forms	Aphrodite, Astarte, Eros, Frigga, Isis
Zodiac signs	Taurus and Libra
Element	Earth
Planetary colour	Green
Planetary metal	Copper
Incense	Rosewood
Flowers	Orchid, rose
Animal	Cat
Bird	Dove

Mars

Planetary influence	Rules machinery, courage, manual dexterity, men, sexual energy, and protection from fire and violence
Day of the week	Tuesday
Archangel	Samuel
God forms	Ares, Mars, Tiw
Zodiac signs	Aries and Scorpio
Element	Fire
Planetary colour	Red
Planetary metal	Iron
Incense	Pine
Flowers	Thistles, nettles
Animal	Ram
Bird	Falcon

Jupiter

Planetary influence	Rules wealth, social status, political power, big business, gambling, legal and insurance matters

Day of the week	Thursday
Archangel	Sachiel
God forms	Dagda, Jupiter, Ptah, Thor, Zeus
Zodiac signs	Sagittarius and Pisces
Element	Fire
Planetary colour	Purple
Planetary metal	Tin
Incense	Cedar
Flower	Lilac
Animal	Bear
Bird	Eagle

Saturn

Planetary influence	Rules property, old people, karma, inheritances, death, agriculture
Day of the week	Saturday
Archangel	Cassiel
God forms	Anubis, Bran, Chronos, the Norns
Zodiac signs	Capricorn and Aquarius
Element	Earth
Planetary colour	Brown/black
Planetary metal	Lead
Incense	Myrrh
Flower	Chrysanthemum
Animal	Tortoise
Bird	Raven

INDEX